Family Tree Pillow
Canvas Game Rug
Treasure Hunt
Personalized T-Shirts, Mugs, Quilts
A Money Nest Egg
People Cookies

Make It Special matches these and hundreds of other wonderfully unique gift ideas to appropriate occasions and shows how even the novice craftsperson can create delightful, inexpensive presents with a personal touch.

All the gift suggestions in this book have come from gifts the authors have given or received or from friends who have told them what gifts they loved. The joy of gift-giving comes through in all the ideas and in the charming line drawings that accompany them. Remember, when you give a filled-with-love gift you've made yourself, it includes the heartwarming message that you care a great deal.

Make It Special

KATHY FAGGELLA is a craft exhibitor, illustrator, and author. She has spent fifteen years teaching arts and crafts to adults and children. Her publications include *Crayons, Crafts and Concepts* and *Concept Cookery.* She is coauthor and illustrator of *Think It Through* and, with Janet Horowitz, of *Partners for Learning.* JANET HOROWITZ is an educational psychologist, creator of children's books, and author of *The Super Sitter Kit.* Janet and Kathy are writers and concept developers for *First Teacher,* a monthly educational publication.

Make It Special
GIFT CREATIONS
FOR ALL OCCASIONS

KATHY FAGGELLA AND JANET HOROWITZ

A PLUME BOOK

NEW AMERICAN LIBRARY

NEW YORK AND SCARBOROUGH, ONTARIO

NAL BOOKS ARE AVAILABLE AT QUANTITY DISCOUNTS
WHEN USED TO PROMOTE PRODUCTS OR SERVICES.
FOR INFORMATION PLEASE WRITE TO PREMIUM MARKETING DIVISION,
NEW AMERICAN LIBRARY, 1633 BROADWAY, NEW YORK, NEW YORK 10019

Copyright © 1986 by Kathy Faggella and Janet Horowitz

Illustrations by Kathy Faggella

PLUME TRADEMARK REG. U.S. PAT. OFF. AND FOREIGN COUNTRIES
REG. TRADEMARK—MARCA REGISTRADA
HECHO EN HARRISONBURG, VA., U.S.A.

SIGNET, SIGNET CLASSIC, MENTOR, ONYX, PLUME, MERIDIAN AND NAL BOOKS are pub-
lished in the United States by New American Library, 1633 Broadway, New York,
New York 10019, in Canada by The New American Library of Canada Limited,
81 Mack Avenue, Scarborough, Ontario M1L 1M8

Library of Congress Cataloging-in-Publication Data
Faggella, Kathy.
  Make it special.

  1. Handicraft. 2. Gifts. I. Horowitz, Janet.
II. Title.
TT157.F26 1986   745.5   86-8350
ISBN 0-452-25746-8 (pbk.)

Designed by Leonard Telesca

First Printing, December, 1986

1 2 3 4 5 6 7 8 9

PRINTED IN THE UNITED STATES OF AMERICA

DEDICATED WITH LOVE AND THANKS

To our parents:
Marie and Joe Poinelli
Muriel and Ernie Blank
who gave us the gifts of life and caring

To our husbands:
Vinny and Len
for their continued support and encouragement
and for giving us
Jimmy and Katie,
Ari, Rachel and Leah—
our GREATEST GIFTS

Contents

Make It Special

Introduction

Mom's birthday
A nephew's graduation
A best friend's wedding
Grandmom and Granddad's anniversary

Each year, the calendar fills up with events and occasions involving special people in our lives. And invariably along with each of these occasions comes the big question: What can I give? Having this book handy will make it a lot easier for you to answer that question from now on.

We think gifts should be useful, unique, and especially appropriate. We also want them to show how much we care. After years of collecting gift suggestions from newspapers and magazines, taking informal surveys among our friends and families, and experimenting with crafts, we've put all our ideas into *Make It Special*. It is a collection of our favorites among the hundreds of creative gifts we've heard about, given, or received.

Make It Special includes gift suggestions for all the milestone occasions. The ideas include store-bought gifts to which you can add a special touch; items that can be put together to make a totally original gift; ordinary gifts that are made extraordinary by the way they are presented; and directions for handmade gifts that you can craft uniquely for special people.

The gifts suggested in *Make It Special* will help you choose (or create) the "just right" presents that will delight your family and friends immediately and inspire warm memories long afterwards. *Make It Special* gifts are as much fun to create as they are to receive. They are a lovely way of showing you care and sharing your love.

Chapter 1

Giving Great Gifts

The special gifts we have received in our lives are usually as easy to remember as the people who gave them to us. Other gifts, although appreciated and enjoyed at the time, fade away in one's memory.

What is special about that great gift that pleases not only at the moment but that is so long remembered? From personal experience and conversations with others, we have found that a great gift can really be ANYTHING if:

- It is just what the person wants.
- It makes the person feel pampered.
- It satisfies a fantasy.
- It fits the occasion.
- It is given as a surprise, perhaps for no occasion at all.
- It fits the person's personality and taste.
- It's totally unique, created with that person or situation in mind. In other words, it can't be bought.

We have also learned that we all have the ability to make our gifts more fun and meaningful. All you have to do is follow the basic guidelines in this chapter and use our book as a guide to putting together and making uniquely personal presents.

Start with the chapter that fits the occasion for which you need a gift, but don't let that limit your choices. Feel free to use any gift suggestion from any category. Mix and match the gift suggestions to the person. A housewarming gift idea might be just perfect for a friend's birthday. Or the ideal gift for *your* teenager might happen to be in the adult birthday section. For the holidays you can use any gift in the book. The anniversary and wedding gifts make great couple gifts, but could also be given to an individual. The possibilities are endless.

What you feel comfortable giving will, of course, depend on your own personality and the relationship you have with the recipient of the gift. A "put together" gift might be the answer if you feel uncomfortable making something from scratch or feel that it will not be appreciated. With some people, you just naturally feel good about handcrafting a gift. With others, you know it is best to buy one.

Consider the gift ideas in this book merely as starting points. You can always add your own personal touches and embellishments.

The Perfect Present

How do you know what a person would really like? Sometimes the answer simply comes from listening for an "I want" or "I'd love" message when a friend indirectly mentions a particular thing he admires. Picking up on these comments really pleases the person because he knows you have paid attention to him, not only in the big, important dialogues but also in little conversations.

Here are some other ways to think through what to give:

1. Try to match personalities with gifts.

Each of us is a one-of-a-kind human being. What makes gift giving a challenge is matching a gift with one particular person.

How do we clue into who a person really is? Here are some useful questions to consider:

- What are this person's special interests, hobbies, or collections?

Art	Music
Carpentry	Painting
Cooking	Pets
Crafts	Photography
Dancing	Politics
Entertaining	Reading
Exercising	Restoring old things
Games	Sports
Gardening/flowers	Theater
History	Travel
Models	Writing

- What are this person's eating preferences?

  Foods (including snacks and ethnic-food preferences)
  Beverages
  Kinds of restaurants

- How does this person like to dress?

Preppy	Favorite colors
Romantic	Jewelry (ears pierced?)
Modern	Makeup
Traditional	Perfumes
Unique	

- What special luxuries does this person enjoy?

  Soaps, bath oils, bubbles
  Manicures
  Pedicures
  Massages

- What style house does this person live in?

  Contemporary
  Colonial
  Victorian

2. Know what gifts are appropriate for the occasion.

There is an etiquette for giving gifts on certain occasions. For example, the milestone occasions such as 25th or 50th anniversaries, 16th, 21st, 40th, 50th or 65th birthdays, or retirements call for gifts of substance. But substance needn't necessarily be costly, although it could be. It just has to be "more"—more unique or more special or just maybe more traditional, such as silver for the 25th and gold for the 50th wedding anniversaries.

Can you break with tradition? Of course, if your present is so clever and pleasing that the expected gifts pale next to it. But appropriateness is still important.

Milestone occasions are often times of transition in people's lives—weddings, graduations, christenings, retirements. Gifts for these occasions should be useful after the celebration. First-marrieds, for instance, can use almost anything from money to silver. (Second-time arounders might enjoy more frivolous gifts for their personal enjoyment.) For high school graduates, look ahead to what they may need in the next few years—from type-writers and computers to transportation.

A gift might not seem useful now, but can still be appropriate. Our thirteen-year-old daughter received a beautiful Seder plate and gorgeous candlesticks on her Bat Mitzvah. Although she had no use for it at the time it was a gift that she will treasure. It will be hers as she grows and will be a constant reminder of her special day. We received a beautiful silver coffee and tea service as a wedding gift. At that time a relative remarked, "You two kids could surely use the money now instead!" Yet, today, we have that service in a prominent place in our home. The money we might have received instead would have been gone long ago. Many keepsake items like the candlesticks and tea service fit the occasion, not necessarily the age of the receiver.

Also consider who is involved. For example, an anniversary gift should be for the two people to share and enjoy, whereas gifts for the individual birthdays should be for the individual themselves, not for their homes or families. How many women have cringed when a husband proudly presented a set of pots and pans as a birthday present? Conversely, we have often made the mistake of giving a rather useful feminine "house" gift such as a lace tablecloth and napkins for an anniversary and heard about it, jokingly, of course, from the outspoken hus-bands.

Birthdays and anniversaries of older people call for a certain type of gift. These occasions call for fun and consumable gifts that can be enjoyed now.

3. Know what you have to offer.

Who are you? Assess your own resources, special talents, skills, strengths and use them whenever you can. Are you good with your hands? Then making a crafted gift would be great for you. With a little know-how and a few directions you can create something wonderful made especially for a particular person. If you have a special talent or skill, you might consider spending time with the person to share your knowledge as a gift. Or your skill as, say, a photographer can be put to use making portraits or photo collections as gifts. Or trade off something you can do with a friend who can do something else. A friend might help cut wood and assemble it into a shelf for you to decorate if you help her make homemade pasta dough.

What do you already own that could become part of a gift? Your old things may make beautiful gifts, particularly for children and teens. For a young child, buy a new jewelry box and fill it with your costume jewelry. A teen may go wild when you give her that original Beatles album that you have grown tired of after twenty years. One woman gave her 20-year-old daughter her old, college days raccoon coat she no longer wore and added a new belt. The daughter loves the fun fur for trendy dressing as well as the fact that it belonged to her mom. Or if your apartment in the city will be empty for a weekend, perhaps your friend would love to stay there (with a refrigerator full of surprises) as part of a gift from you.

Planning Ahead

You can avoid a frantic, last-minute effort to find the "right" gift with a little ahead-of-time organization. The following strategies have made life easier for us.

1. Keep a gift file.
When you are listening and observing, make mental notes. To free your mind of all you've collected, jot the gift ideas down. (Just by the process of writing a note and rereading it you've put it more permanently into your memory.) But after many years of losing little slips of paper and backs of grocery lists and messing up the covers of telephone books, we've come to the conclusion that a file of some sort is best.

A gift file can be:

- A box into which you've thrown all those little slips of paper
- A notebook
- 3 × 5 note cards in a file box

What else can go into your file? Perhaps great gift ideas you've heard about or advertisements for intriguing items. Most of us read a great many periodicals and newspapers. We see products advertised and read about new things on the market. When one of these things strikes you as special, clip it out of the magazine or newspaper and put it into your file. At some future time you will be able to make a match between a person and that item. It may also serve as a stimulus for another great idea or put-together combination.

The same is true of catalogs. They are wonderful gift inspirations. You can order from them or just get ideas from them. They also offer you the added incentive of being able to choose a gift, in the correct price range and size, right in the comfort of your home. We are particularly fond of the catalogs that have showrooms where you can look over the quality of a gift you have already chosen and then pick it up on the spot. See pages 215–218 for a mailing list for a variety of catalogs.

2. Keep a gift box.

One of the best gift-giving tips we can pass on is the gift-box idea. For years we have kept a cardboard carton in the closet for jewelry, toys, knickknacks, stationery, and household goodies. We've purchased an item:

- When we felt it was unique
- When we just had to have it because it was irresistible
- When it was on sale—best are the stores going out of business that offer 50 percent off.

We keep these items together for those little spur-of-the-moment gifts, your children's friends' birthday parties, going to someone's house, and any occasion where you can fit a gift to a person. Many times we have saved ourselves hours and lots of tension by not having to run out at the last minute to pick something up. Including unique and beautiful cards in the gift box also helps.

3. Keep track of important dates.

January may find the more organized of us transferring birthdays and anniversaries from last year's date book/calendar to the new year's date book/calendar. But for most of us a better solution is a permanent calendar.

A permanent calendar lists the days of each month without the specific date number coordinated to a day of the week. Therefore, it can be used year after year.

On this permanent calendar you can record all birthdays, anniversaries, births, and weddings with the year written in. This calendar makes it easy to know what anniversary someone is celebrating or how old the baby will be. It is lovely to send a greeting on the first anniversary if you attended the wedding.

A permanent calendar also offers you the option of jotting down what you've given as a gift. This is useful:

- To continue to add another piece to a collection
- To renew a subscription
- To avoid a duplication
- To give you a clue for the next gift

4. Make lists.

If we have listened and observed, clipped and collected, then making a list of gift ideas should be easy.

An "association list" can be especially helpful. Begin by writing down the name of each person to whom you plan to give a gift. Place the names in a column down the left side of a piece of paper. Now read off each name aloud and quickly jot down the FIRST word you associate with that person. Next, fill in general gift ideas using the broad categories you've established. Then use your association list to make connections to specific gifts. For example:

Joanne—business—something for the rising young executive; a leather business card file to put cards in that she needs to refer to on a regular basis.

Vin—out of doors—something to make the time he spends working outside more fun; a slip on radio with earphones to use while mowing and gardening.

Susan—reflective—something for herself; an astrological reading.

Marie—sentimental—something homemade for the house; a stenciled and quilted family tree pillow.

Just remember our formula for success:

YOU + THIS BOOK = GREAT GIFTS!

Chapter 2

Basic Craft Techniques and Tips

You may not think of yourself as an artisan of wood, clay, paint or cloth, but if the desire is there, you can make wonderful items to give to those you love.

This chapter includes all the basic hints for techniques that will help you create the craft gifts within this book. You can also adapt the basic techniques to personalize any gift, to make it more useful, or humorous, or to make use of what you already have on hand.

Handy Equipment

Ruler with a metal edge

Yardstick

Tape measure

Sewing machine with a zigzag stitch

Hammer

Assortment of nails

Cross cut hand saw

Hand drill with assortment of bits

Jigsaw

Assortment of sandpapers

Fabric cutting scissors

Craft knife (X-acto)

Assortment of fine-tipped, permanent marking pens

Assortment of small jars of acrylic paints

Liquid, brush-on poly-urethane (Zip-Guard is one brand name)

Assortment of different-sized brushes

Glue

Working with Glues

The term *glue* can include everything from mucilage to white glue to hot glue to rubber cement to super glues. Each has a slightly different function.

- Aleene's "Tacky" white glue is a thick, wonderful glue for quick adherence.
- Elmer's glue is thinner, water soluble, yet dries shiny and transparent.
- Elmer's wood glue is best to use on wood.
- Mucilage is best used on paper. We have discovered that if it is watered down with a ratio of three parts glue to one part water, then brushed over the back side of a sheet of paper, and allowed to dry completely, the glue acts like the glue on a postage stamp. All you need to do is moisten it.
- Hot glue is produced by heating a glue stick in a glue gun (Thermogrip is one brand) and squeezing the trigger to obtain a hot liquid with quick adherence. It is best used on paper and fabric. It adheres two pieces of wood, but may not be permanent. It does not adhere as well to metals.
- Rubber cement's big advantage is that it can be peeled off with a gum eraser. It is used only on paper and is not permanent over a long period of time.
- Super glues and cements are strong holding and quite permanent.

Using Our Patterns

How to Enlarge Patterns

Each pattern is drawn on a grid with the scale 1 inch = 1 square.

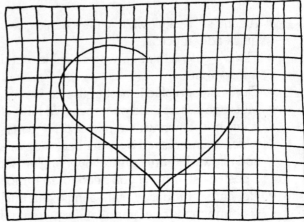

YOU NEED:

Paper (typing, newspaper, tracing, brown grocery bags opened up, reverse side of decorative wrapping)

12-inch ruler or yardstick

Pencil

YOU DO:

1. Count the number of squares along the horizontal and vertical edges of the grid from which you are copying.

2. Mark with the pencil the horizontal and vertical edges of your blank paper at 1-inch intervals, making sure your paper is large enough to accommodate the grid you are reproducing.

3. Draw parallel lines, using the ruler and a pencil, to make the grid with horizontal and vertical lines 1 inch apart. Now each square is 1 inch long and 1 inch wide.

4. Reproduce the pattern onto the grid by copying the lines of the pattern square by square.

5. Pattern is now drawn to the exact size you will need. Cut out pattern.

How to Transfer Enlarged Pattern to Fabric

YOU NEED:
Straight pins
#2 pencil or chalk or transfer pen
Fabric
Masking tape
Enlarged paper pattern

YOU DO:
1. Lay fabric on a hard surface. Tape around fabric's edges to hold tightly.

2. Position pattern on fabric. Pin in place.

3. Trace around pattern with a #2 pencil or piece of chalk. A transfer pen will mark a line that can later be removed by washing fabric in cold water.

How to Transfer a Pattern from the Book to Fabric

YOU NEED:
Tracing paper
#2 pencil
Scissors or craft knife

YOU DO:
1. Place tracing paper over pattern in book.

2. Trace around pattern with pencil.

3. Cut out pattern.

How to Transfer Designs from Book to Fabric

YOU NEED:
Tracing paper

#2 pencil

YOU DO:

1. Place tracing paper over design in book. Trace around design with pencil.

2. Turn paper over and cover design (as you see it through the paper) with thick #2 pencil marks. To do this, hold the pencil on its side and rub point on paper.

3. Turn the paper to the right side.

4. Retrace the design with pencil onto desired surface. Markings on back will "print" your design.

Basic Sewing Stitches

Slip Stitch

Use this stitch to close an opening, such as the opening used to stuff a pillow. Sew back and forth from one edge to the opposite, just catching one layer of fabric on the underneath side of the fold. When pulled closed, the stitching is barely visible.

Quilting

Use this stitch to secure batting between top and bottom fabrics. Use only one strand of 100% cotton thread. Stitch goes straight down through all fabric layers (needle is perpendicular to floor) and is pushed up from bottom so that length of each stitch is ⅛-inch long. (Never quilt by pushing the needle through several long stitches as in a running stitch.)

Running Stitch

Use this stitch for general sewing to attach layers of fabric together. Long lengths between stitches are basting stitches and can be removed easily. Short lengths between stitches are tighter and more secure.

Appliqué

Use this stitch to attach one piece of fabric on top of another. The stitch goes back and forth between the two fabrics, in tiny lengths, catching one layer of fabric on each piece. This stitch should always be done in single strand, with the same color thread as the appliqué piece; it is barely visible.

Machine appliqué attaches the raw edge of an overlapped piece of fabric with a thick zigzag stitch.

Embroidery

Use these stitches as decorative work. Use embroidery thread in your choice of color. Thread is generally split into three strands and cut into 18-inch lengths for more manageability.

Basic Sewing Techniques

Pinning

Use common pins and pin perpendicular to the edge of fabric. In this way you can avoid having to baste fabrics together, because most sewing machines will sew directly over pins when they are placed perpendicular, as opposed to parallel, to the edge.

Cutting

Use pinking shears whenever possible to keep fabric edges from unraveling.

Clipping Curves

Use this technique whenever you have sewn around a curve and need to turn the fabric object inside out. Omitting this clipping will cause puckering of the fabric when turned. Use tips of scissors and clip in a stroke perpendicular to the edge into the fabric, almost to the stitching line.

Gathering

To gather a length of fabric into soft, irregular folds, you must first machine sew or hand baste a running stitch (long length) across the entire length of fabric. Leave about 6 inches of thread at each end. Gently pull bobbin thread in machine stitch or basting thread in hand stitch, creating gathered folds as you pull. Tie machine threads together to hold. Knot both ends of thread if using a hand-basting stitch.

Quilting

Quilt piece must be stretched tightly over an embroidery hoop or quilting frame. Securing batting between two layers of fabric can be accomplished in two ways. (1) Use 100% cotton single-strand thread. Begin quilting stitch by making a small knot at end of thread and yanking it gently through one layer of fabric. Knot is therefore concealed inside quilt. Continue quilting stitch. (2) Avoid quilting altogether by fastening the quilt together at a few specific points with yarn or ribbon. Secure lengths of ribbon or yarn onto top layer by sewing them on with needle and thread pushed through all layers.

Basic Stitches

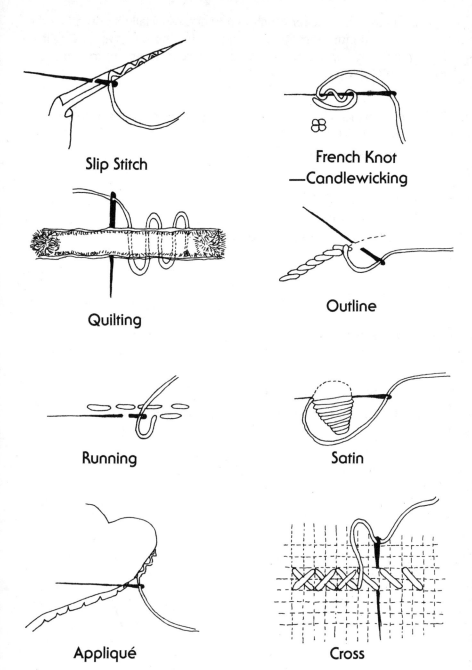

Slip Stitch

French Knot
—Candlewicking

Quilting

Outline

Running

Satin

Appliqué

Cross

Small Soft-Sculpture Face

These add a clever touch to any gift, especially if you make the soft sculpture resemble the person to whom you are giving it. As with any soft sculpture, some practice is necessary to make it look as you want it to look!

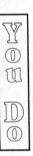

one 4-inch circle of scrap hosiery or flesh-colored interlock polyknit fabric

needle and beige thread

two tiny seed beads

a handful of polyester stuffing

yarn for hair

makeup—blush-on, lipstick

1. Use needle and beige thread to sew a running stitch along edge of circle about ¼ inch in, and pull gently to gather into a bag shape.

2. Stuff tightly with polyester stuffing.

3. Pull thread tightly and secure with a knot.

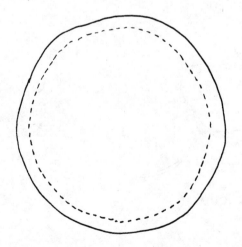

4. Make features by pushing needle from back "hole" to smooth front.

Nose: Push needle through head to center of "face." Taking tiny stitches, go back and forth from one side of the nose to the other. Each time use needle to lift stuffing into nose section. Finish nose by taking a stitch into each "nostril" and pulling it to back of head.

Eyes: Push needle through head to side of nose. Place a tiny bead on needle. Sew through eye position to other eye position. Place other bead on needle and sew back and forth three or four times to secure bead. Push needle to back of head and secure.

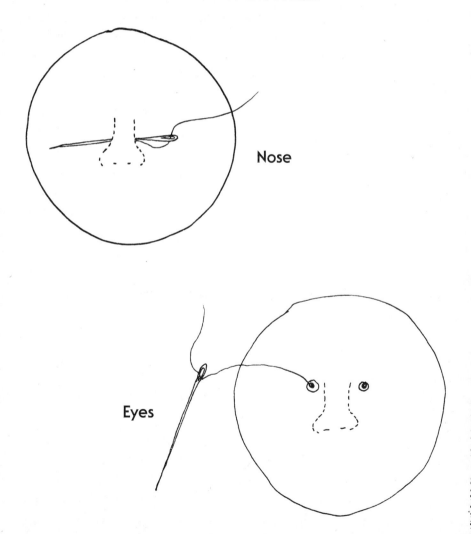

Nose

Eyes

Mouth: Push needle from back of head to a side of the mouth position. Take long running stitches to form an upturned grin. (See step A.) Pull slightly and push needle back through head. Secure tightly. Push needle to front just under first stitches on mouth. Push needle back and forth from under first line of stitches to a grin line ¼ inch below. Push up some polyester stuffing to make a "pouting" lip. Make lips thicker in center of mouth. (See step B.)

5. Add yarn hair, in any style, by sewing on individual curls or strands of straight hair. Sew on loops for a curly effect.

6. Use these soft-sculpture heads in many ways. You can vary size of each head by increasing or decreasing size of circle. Attach them by sewing or gluing with a hot glue gun.

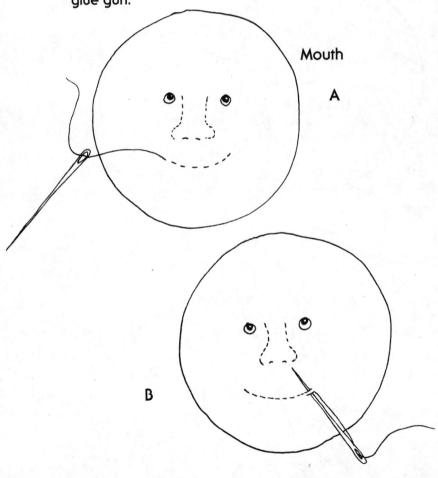

Mouth

A

B

Decorative Techniques

Stenciling

This technique uses paint on fabric. It is best used when straight, even lines of paint are needed. It is permanent, and there is very little build-up of paint on the fabric. The finished product will have an appealing Early American look.

YOU NEED

Sheets of waxed stencil paper (available in most craft stores)

Round bristled stencil brushes

Stencil paints

Craft knife

Masking tape

Newspaper

Old magazine

Ball-point pen

YOU DO

1. Place waxed stencil paper over picture or pattern to be copied. Tape into place.

2. Trace picture with ball-point pen onto waxed stencil paper. (See step A.)

A

3. Remove paper and place it on magazine. Use craft knife to cut on traced outlines of picture or pattern. (See step B.) Remember, you will keep the whole paper and discard the inside pieces.

4. You want good, clean lines when cutting. If by chance you cut into the whole stencil paper at a corner, you must tape the cut on both sides of the paper so your paint will not run or "bleed" into your print.

5. Place your stencil on fabric. Tape stencil and fabric to hard surface covered with four layers of newspaper.

6. Dip brush into small amount of paint. Bristles should be covered on tips only. Tap excess paint on scrap paper.

7. Stencil by tapping the brush straight up and down, working from the outer edge of the stencil in toward the center. Traditionally a stenciled pattern is darkest at the edges and leaves some background color showing through at the center. (See step C.)

8. If colors in the pattern are to be stenciled very closely together, you may have to make separate stencils for each color. However, you can also mask with tape any section already painted in order to stencil paint with another color. In either case, allow one color of paint to dry completely.

9. Let entire stenciled pattern dry thoroughly, then iron on reverse side of fabric to set.

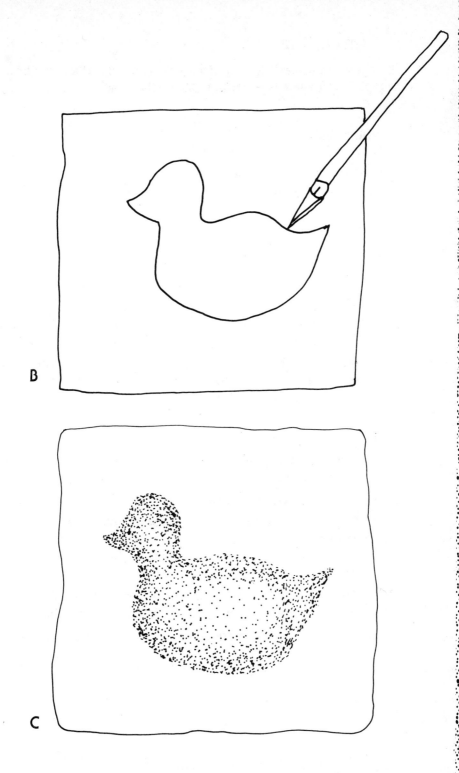

B

C

Transfer Crayons

Fabric crayons are dyes in stick form. You transfer the dye from a picture drawn on paper to fabric by the heat of an iron.

YOU NEED

Crayola fabric crayons (available in most art and craft stores)

Clean paper (typing, newsprint)

All or part synthetic fabric (cotton/polyester is fine)

Iron

Newspapers

1 sheet clean, white paper for each design to be transferred

YOU DO

1. Draw a design or picture on clean paper with fabric crayons.

2. When drawing words, numbers, or designs that are most definitely left-right, make sure you draw them *backward*. They will be transferred onto fabric the correct way.

3. Place fabric on short stack of newspapers.

4. Place crayoned design down on top of fabric. Make sure crayoned surface is in contact with fabric.

5. Place a piece of clean white paper over all.

6. Set iron at "cotton" setting and gently place over design. Hold design paper and fabric firmly with free hand. Slowly move iron all around design, making sure paper does not move.

7. Check under a corner of the design paper after 30 seconds. If color is vibrant and clear, slowly check the rest.

8. Remove iron and design paper when transfer is completed.

Transfer Paints

These paints are directly applied to paper. Allow them to dry thoroughly, then iron onto synthetic fabric. Polyester is best. Cotton/polyester is okay, but some fading occurs after washing.

YOU NEED
DEKA iron-on transfer paints

Synthetic fabric (polyester)

2 sheets clean, white paper

Fine-lined (0–00) brushes

YOU DO
1. Use a brush to paint a design on paper. Design may be outlined first in paint and then filled in, if desired. Allow each color to dry thoroughly before using another color.
2. Place fabric on a sheet of newspaper on ironing board. Place painted design paper face down onto fabric. Cover with a clean piece of paper.
3. Set iron to "cotton" and place over design. Do not move iron. Design should be set in 45 to 60 seconds. Test by picking up a corner while holding the design firmly on the fabric.
4. Remove iron and design paper when transfer is completed.

Fabric Paints

There are a number of paints on the market that will adhere directly to fabric. We use either stencil paints such as Fab Tex by Stencil Ease or regular acrylics such as Accent colors. You can thin thick acrylics with an addition of gloss polymer to make it spread more easily.

Apply fabric paints with a stiff acrylic brush. It is far easier to apply fabric paints to stiffer fabrics such as canvas, linen, duck, broadcloth, and denim, than to knits such as T-shirts.

Chapter 3

Gifts for Babies

One of the greatest joys in life is experiencing the beginning of a new one. If anticipation adds to the pleasure, then nature has given us nine months of it! The about-to-be parents use the time to prepare themselves for the new family member. That leaves the rest of us to plan how we will greet the child. A baby gift is a joy to give and, if the gift is special, a memorable way to share in the event.

༕ Put-together Suggestions ༕

Gifts for the firstborn are usually easy to think of because the parents need so many practical items. All you have to do is add a creative touch. Here are some ideas to inspire you.

- Clothing for the baby from the parent's alma mater. Write to the school's store for a catalog.
- A hand-me-down item with a new gift item. For instance, give your child's carriage with a new set of carriage sheets or quilt, crib with a new night-light or intercom, playpen or stroller with new stimulation toys.
- Calendar or baby book/journal to record events of baby's first year. Promise to take and contribute the necessary photos.
- Toiletry items stuffed into a hanging shoe bag.

- A baby tub filled with bath items such as a hooded bath towel, puppet washcloth, and water toy.
- A "new" family portrait. Take the picture yourself and frame it.
- A baby carrier for their bike—installed, of course.
- Sitter pad or memo board with list of great sitters.
- Bottle of champagne, soothing classical music tapes, flowers, gourmet meal and nibbles. Send over one or more of the above after complaints of sleepless nights.
- How-to parenting books or magazine subscription with your list of other good resources and support systems, and an introduction to an infant parent group.
- Hire or be a maid-for-a-day. Or take the older siblings out.
- Design and have printed the baby announcement or thank-you cards.
- A wall mural painted by you or a hired artist.
- A collaged photo of baby's first year. Photograph baby on the last day of each month of baby's first year. Assemble the 12 photos in succession and frame.
- Give a collector's item or gift that will be special to the child as he grows up:

   A child's set of china
   A real tree planted in their yard or a bonsai for apartment dwellers
   An heirloom necklace. Begin by giving either 14K gold beads or sterling silver or cultured pearls to be added onto for each succeeding birthday.

- A baby carrying basket. The parents can use it for the baby; then the child can use it for carrying dolls and animals.
- A U.S. savings bond or a share of stock to which you can add on future birthdays.
- A baby quilt with toy pocket. Sew a pocket (large enough to hold a small stuffed soft toy) onto a purchased quilt and include the toy.
- A plain canvas bag packed with a book of jokes, a novel, a box of special chocolates, a bottle of liquor, a mug, tea bags, cocoa mixes, and a TV Guide. (Optional: on the bag write "2 A.M. Survival Kit. Good luck.")

Counted Cross-stitched Bib & "Burpie"
Diaper-bag & receiving blanket

Hankie Bonnet

One lacy handkerchief folded and tacked with a little thread can become a beautiful keepsake bonnet for baby. Give it for the christening. Years later, the tacking threads can be removed so the child can use it for her wedding—or give it to his bride as "something old."

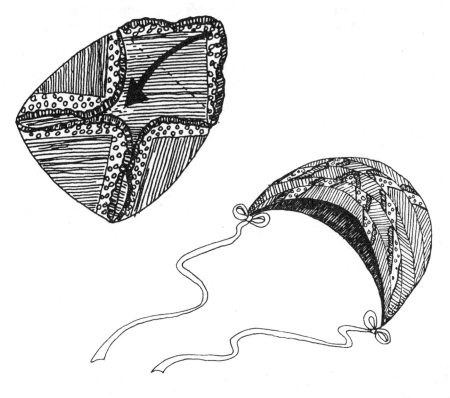

One 12-inch lacy square white handkerchief
Pins
Needle and thread
1 yard white satin ⅛ to ¼-inch ribbon

1. Lay the handkerchief on a flat surface.

2. Fold all four corners to the center and pin together. Tack down corners in center with needle and thread.

3. Turn square over so lacy edges are on the bottom.

4. Accordian fold the square five times, starting with one fold up along one edge, *not* a corner. Pin the two ends. These ends will be at baby's ears, whereas the rest of hankie will expand open. Tack securely at both ends.

5. Cut the ribbon in half. Tie a tiny bow on one end of each piece. Tack the bows to each sewn end of the bonnet. Use the loose ties to tie under baby's chin.

Crib Mobile

A mobile strung across an infant's crib provides visual stimulation and promotes motor development. Unlike many beautiful commercial mobiles, this one is not a look-but-don't touch model. The toys can be taken off and given to the child.

45-inch long piece of ribbon (grosgrain or embroidered)

1⅔ yards of ¼-inch ribbon

2 sets of Velcro tabs

5 infant toys such as rubber teething ring, stuffed animal, feeding spoon with a loop, rattle, bathtub toy

Needle and thread

1. Turn under ½ inch of each end of the 45-inch long ribbon and stitch in place. Sew one Velcro tab in place at the two ends. Sew the other tabs 4 inches in from each end.

2. Cut the ¼-inch ribbon into 12-inch pieces.

3. Sew each piece of ¼-inch ribbon onto the long 45-inch ribbon by tacking it down on the middle (6 inches from each end). Each piece can be placed about 8 inches apart.

4. Tightly tie a toy to each ribbon.

5. Attach to crib by suspending from rail to rail and firmly pressing the Velcro tabs together.

"On the Day I Was Born" (a scrapbook)

Have you ever wondered what life must have been like when you were born? What were the fashions like? What was happening in the sports world? What books were people reading?

This gift will be treasured by new parents because it will answer questions like that for their baby. One day, the child will treasure this gift, too!

1 cloth-covered scrapbook
1 newspaper from the day of child's birth
Glue
Markers
A sheet of waxed stencil paper
Stencil craft knife
Masking tape
Ball-point pen
Stencil paint (one-color)
Stencil brush

1. Use markers to title pages; the first page is titled "Headlines."

2. Cut out major headlines on first page and glue under that category.

3. Continue to clip and glue samples of the newspaper into categories like the following:

   sports   fashions
   comics   arts
   movies   food sales
   jobs—classified

4. Place sheet of stencil paper over title in this book. Trace with ball-point pen. Cut out letters with craft knife.

5. Tape waxed stencil paper to front of scrapbook. Stencil in title with brush and paint.

6. You may wish to stencil in the child's name and birth date. (For detailed stencil instruction see pages 21–22).

ON THE DAY I WAS BORN

Baby Bead Bracelet

Here is a lovely, inexpensive gift you can whip up in no time at all for the new mom. This baby bead bracelet will become a keepsake with the baby's name and birth date on it. (It's also a nice gift to give to a female infant when she gets older.) Present it to the new mom in the hospital!

1 bracelet kit which includes wire, a closure, and two crip beads. All these materials can be found in a craft store.

Glass letter beads to spell out baby's name and date of birth

4 mm glass (or plastic) colored beads. You may want to choose pink and white for a girl, blue and white for a boy, or mom's favorite colors.

Tweezers or needle-nose pliers to squeeze crip beads together

1. Measure the wire to go around your wrist. Add 1 inch more. Cut.

2. Attach fastener to one end of wire. Follow kit directions.

3. Lay out your design. Place a colored bead between each letter bead. Add extra beads on either end. Leave ½ inch of wire showing on free end.

4. Attach free end to fastener.

Baby-Carriage Quilt

This tiny quilt can be assembled in very little time. Later, at a shower or small party, complete it by passing out blank pieces of paper for everyone to sign and draw on simple designs with fabric crayons. Iron the designs onto the blank squares in the quilt.

1¾ yards solid blue fabric (45 inches wide)

¼ yard coordinated pink/blue/yellow calico print

¼ yard solid white fabric (must be part synthetic fabric)

Needle and thread

Pins

Cotton quilt batting

2 yards ⅛-inch color-coordinated ribbon

Crayola fabric crayons

6 × 6 inch squares white typing paper

Iron

1. Cut one piece of the solid blue fabric into 25 × 35 inch size. This is quilt backing.

2. Cut blue fabric into following strip sizes:

> 4 strips, 3 inches × 31 inches
> 2 strips, 3 inches × 25 inches
> 9 strips, 3 inches × 7 inches

3. Cut calico print fabric into six 6-inch squares.

4. Cut solid white fabric into six 6-inch squares.

How to Assemble the Quilt

(Use ½-inch seam allowances throughout.)

1. Sew three columns of squares and blue strips as follows:

> column one—calico square, 3 × 7 inch blue strip
> white square, 3 × 7 inch blue strip
> calico square, 3 × 7 inch blue strip
> white square

column two—white square, 3 × 7 inch blue strip
calico square, 3 × 7 inch blue strip
white square, 3 × 7 inch blue strip
calico square
column three—repeat column one

2. Connect by pinning and then sewing columns one and two with one 3 × 31 inch long blue strip.

3. Connect the above to column three with one 3 × 31 inch long blue strip.

4. Sew one 3 × 31 inch long blue strip to each right and left side of assembled piece.

5. Sew one 3 × 25 inch blue strip across top of piece.

6. Sew one 3 × 25 inch blue strip across bottom of piece.

7. Place finished quilt front face up on hard surface.

8. Cover with blue fabric backing face down on top of it.

9. Cut cotton quilt batting to exact size of quilt and place over the pieces.

10. Pin through all three layers, then sew ½ inch in from edges around three sides and one half of last side.

11. Clip corners and turn quilt right side out. Slip stitch opening.

12. Cut ⅛-inch ribbon into 12-inch sections. Tie each into a bow and tack through all layers with needle and thread into center of each calico square. This will provide not only decoration but will hold quilt batting in place.

How to Complete Quilt

Draw or print with fabric crayons on paper squares. *Remember,* lettering must be done in reverse. Iron designs onto each blank square.

Baby-Carriage Quilt

Name Pillows

Each child's name has a significance to the family. Honor the baby and his family by making these large cuddly pillows that spell out the baby's name. Color coordinate them to the baby's room.

Enlarged pattern (see illustration)

Chalk

1 yard of solid, calico, or gingham fabric (this will make 4 letters)

12 ounces polyester stuffing

Needle and thread (or sewing machine)

1. Enlarge the letters of the child's name. Each letter is 14″ tall and 10″ wide. (See patterns on pages 39–42.) Cut out.
2. Trace around pattern with chalk on fabric.
3. Double fabric with right sides together and cut each letter out.
4. Stitch ½ inch from all edges of fabric, leaving bottom section open to turn.
5. Clip into curves. Clip tips from corners.
6. Turn letter right side out.
7. You can stitch inside negative spaces (as in the B, P, O, etc.) and trim away excess fabric with sharp, pointed scissors. Or you can just stitch the fabric together at those points and not stuff there.
8. Stuff tightly with polyester stuffing. Use an unsharpened pencil to get into corners or distant areas.
9. Slip stitch closed.

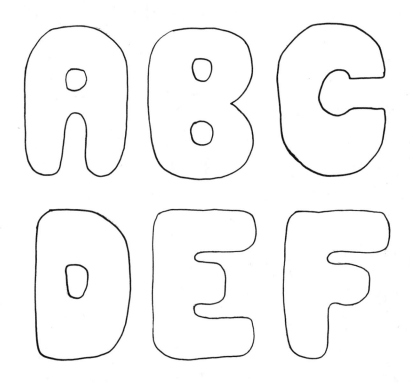

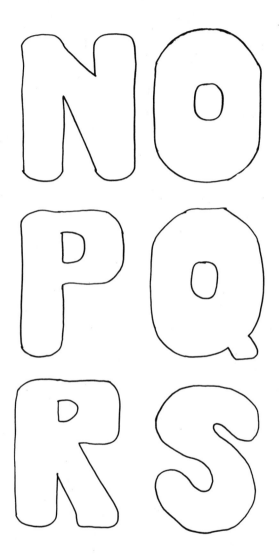

TUV
WX
YZ

Commemorative Pincushion

During Colonial times, it was traditional to give a beautifully decorated pincushion to the parents of a newborn baby girl. This pincushion commemorated the child's birth and was later used by her.

You can carry on the tradition with a lovely, lace-covered pincushion. You might want to combine it with a thoroughly modern gift.

⅛ yard satin fabric in white or pale pink

One 6-inch square doily (or round if that is the only one available). Find one at a tag sale, in an antique store, or purchase a new one or use a lacy handkerchief.

White embroidery thread and large-eye embroidery needle

1 yard of ⅛-inch white satin ribbon

Needle and thread

Polyester stuffing

1. For the square doily, cut two pieces of satin 6-inches square. For a round doily, cut two satin circles 5 inches in diameter.

2. On one piece of satin, embroider, in outline stitch, child's initials and date of birth. For example: KJD 5/2/84 would be placed in the center of square or circular piece of satin.

3. Place two pieces of satin right sides together. Sew around four sides, ½ inch in, leaving a 2-inch opening. Clip corners, turn and stuff tightly with polyester stuffing. Slip stitch the opening closed. (For the round pincushion, sew around circumference ½ inch in, leaving a 2-inch opening. Clip all around curves. Turn fabric right side out and stuff tightly with polyester stuffing. Slip stitch the opening closed.)

4. Place doily or handkerchief tightly over the top of pincushion. (It is perfectly fine for lacy edges to overhang
the pincushion). Weave ribbon through doily or lacy
areas around edge of pincushion. Tie both ends in a
flowing bow. Tack down the doily on pincushion with
needle and thread. (If you are using a lace handkerchief
that is much larger than the pincushion, you may have to
tack down pleats around the center point of the handkerchief on the pincushion.)

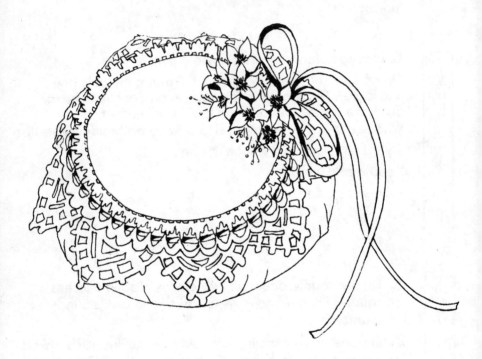

Chapter

Gifts for Toddlers

The 1-to-3-year-old child is known as the Great Explorer. Just watch him play with the telephone and your pots and pans, rushing about from one activity to the next and learning by tasting and handling things.

Make sure that any items you give to a toddler do not have sharp edges, pointed parts, or tiny detachable parts. Watch out for items that could pinch skin or catch hair. Make sure any long cords are shortened so he can't strangle on them. Read labels to ensure you have products that are nontoxic.

Gifts for toddlers should satisfy their wonderful need to explore the world and discover their physical skills. Art supplies, bubbles, play doughs, dress-up clothes, dolls, puppets, and any of the push-and-pull, riding toys, slides, and swings make good gifts at this stage.

Put-together Suggestions

- Tub toys (boats, floaters, squirters, cups, corks, pumpers) in a mesh bag or wrapped in a special bath towel.
- A set of hats in a big round storage box.
- A toy shelf with a manipulative toy wrapped up with it such as nesting boxes, snap lock beads, interlocking blocks, hammer and peg workbench.

- A kiddie pool, new bathing suit, and safety swim vest.
- A popular stuffed animal or doll plus matching eating utensils, dishes, or sheets.
- A silver monogrammed piggy bank with some change to put into it.
- A piece of furniture or a room accessory for the child to use as he grows; for example, a bookshelf with a special book that you've signed and dated.

Soft Baby

Soft Baby is a doll made from a child's own infant stretch suit. You stuff the suit until it is as soft as a pillow, add a head and features that resemble the child, and you have a gift that will be enjoyed as a toy and treasured as a keepsake for many years.

1 infant stretch suit (0–6 months) with a zipper, if possible

12 ounces polyester stuffing

¼ yard interlock polyknit fabric (flesh colored)

Regular needle and thread

Embroidery needle and thread (match with child's eyes) and pink thread for lips

Yarn for hair

Child's infant-sized bonnet or cap

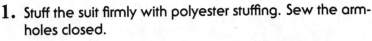

1. Stuff the suit firmly with polyester stuffing. Sew the arm-holes closed.

2. Close the zipper or stitch closed along the snaps.

3. Cut a circle with a 10-inch diameter from polyknit fabric.

4. With thread, sew a running stitch along edge of circle about ¼ inch in and pull gently to gather into a bag shape. Stuff tightly with polyester stuffing and pull gathered thread closed. Secure with a knot.

5. *To make the nose:* Thread needle with a long piece of single-strand thread. Secure with a knot at base of neck and push needle through head to center of face. Taking tiny stitches, go back and forth from one side of the nose to the other. Pull slightly on thread and poke needle into center of nose, lifting some of the polyester stuffing into the area. Finish nose by taking a stitch into each "nostril," and pushing needle to base of neck. Secure tightly.

6. *To make the eyes:* Thread needle with embroidery thread (three strands). Secure with a knot at base of neck and push needle through head to eye position. Stitch a few satin stitches for eye and push needle to other eye position. *Pull slightly on thread to recess eyes on face.* Stitch a few satin stitches for second eye and push needle through head to neck, pulling slightly to recess that eye. Secure with a knot.

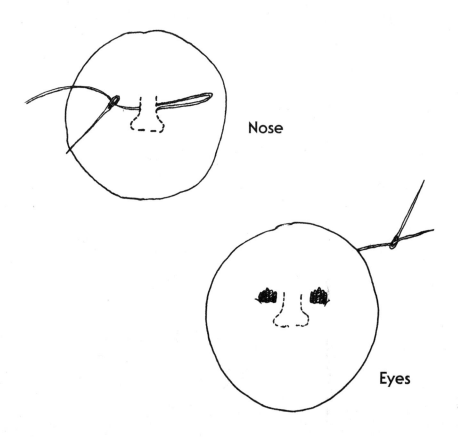

Nose

Eyes

7. *To make the mouth:* Thread needle with four strands of embroidery thread. Secure with a knot at base of neck and push through head to mouth position. Take two long stitches—one from the outer corner of the mouth to center, dipping the line slightly and the other from the opposite corner of the mouth to the same center point. Pull slightly as you push needle back to base of neck and secure with a knot.

8. *To make hair:* Thread a long piece of yarn through large-eye needle. It should be single strand. Secure at base of the back of head with a knot. Now make close rows of yarn loops about 2 inches long over all head for hair. Sew one loop, then secure it with a tight stitch, then sew another loop and another tight stitch. Head should have a thick covering of yarn loops. You may keep hair in loops or cut each loop with a scissors.

9. With needle and thread, sew the head to the stuffed body. Secure tightly.

10. Tie on bonnet to head or sew on cap.

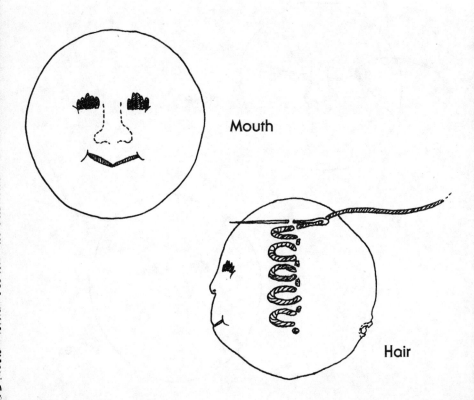

Mouth

Hair

Cap

Fabric Book

Even now, our young daughter loves to "reread" the fabric book I gave her and hear about how she would suck her thumb when she touched the piece of satin that was sewn onto one page.

¼ yard of 4 different tiny-print calicos

½ yard light-colored canvas or canvaslike cloth (you'll need a piece 11 × 17 inches)

Needle and thread

Yarn scraps

Ruler

Items to put into book can include:

—*clothespin*
—*piece of large ball fringe*
—*patches of satin, velvet, leather, felt, burlap*

—*extra-large button*
—*extra-large safety pin*
—*plastic toys*
—*large plastic paper clip*

You Do

1. Measure and cut two pieces of the same print calico to 8 × 11 inches. Place right sides together and sew ½ inch from edges along the two 8-inch long sides and one 11-inch side. Clip corners and turn right side out. This is one "page." (See step A.)

2. Repeat step 1 using two more pieces of the same print calico used above. Continue to sew up two "pages" from each of the four pieces of calico.

3. Cut the piece of canvas or canvaslike cloth to 11 × 17 inches. This will be the cover.

4. Fold all edges of canvas under ½ inch and topstitch ⅜ inches in from edges all around. (See step B.)

5. Use 1-inch scrap pieces of calico to cut out letters in child's name.

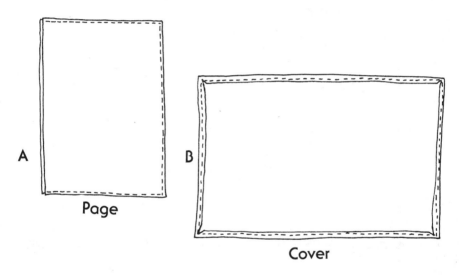

A

Page

B

Cover

One-Inch Scrap Fabric—Pencil in Lines and Cut

6. Machine appliqué the letters across center front of canvas cover. (Remember, front cover is 8½ × 11 inches. It is the folded size, not the whole piece.)

7. Place folded cover around the pages, which have been stacked together with the one unsewn raw edge of each page facing center fold of inside canvas cover. (See step C.) Make sure all pages are lined up evenly. Cover will extend ¼ inch beyond pages.

8. Topstitch on cover ½ inch in from folded side to secure cover to pages. Reinforce stitching by stitching again right over first line. (See step D.)

9. Sew patches of various fabrics to each page. (You can sew directly through the page to attach two pieces.)

10. Sew on short pieces of yarn scraps to tie on toys or a clothespin.

11. Sew on button very tightly.

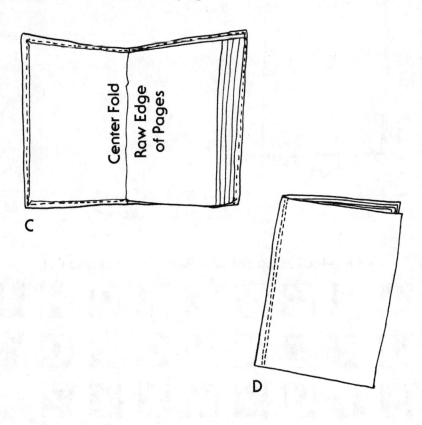

Center Fold

Raw Edge of Pages

C

D

"Let's Eat Out" Kit

This carrying mat—filled with a few toys and eating utensils—lets parents take their toddler to a restaurant without spoiling the fun for themselves. Open up this canvas carrier to use as a place mat. Then close its Velcro fastening so that toys and other items can be transported with ease.

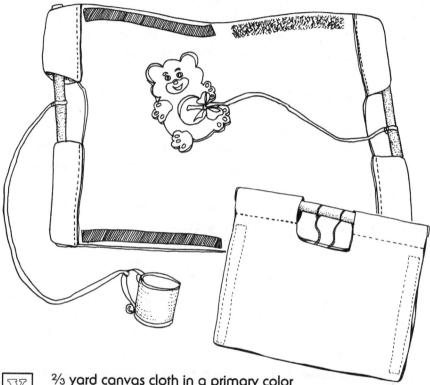

You Need

⅔ yard canvas cloth in a primary color

One 1½-inch-thick × 3-foot-long wooden dowel

One ¾-inch wide × 1½ feet strip of Velcro (available in fabric stores)

Choice of some of the following:

—rubber teething pretzel
—plastic handle spoon
—covered cup that doesn't tip
—plastic figure (toy)
—bib

3 yards ¼-inch ribbon

Ruler

Pins

1. Cut canvas cloth into two pieces each 13 × 22 inches.

2. On each piece of canvas, measure along the 13-inch sides and mark 5 inches from either end. You will have 3 inches left at the center. At the 5-inch mark, measure 4 inches into the fabric. You will have created a rectangle 3 × 4 inches in size. Cut out this rectangle on each side of each piece of fabric.

3. Place right sides of two canvas pieces together and sew ½ inch in from all edges. Leave a 4-inch opening along center section of *one* 22-inch side. Clip all corners and cut slots into interior corners.

4. Turn carrying mat right side out, making sure you poke all corners out. *Wash mat and dry.* This will cause slight shrinkage. Iron well.

5. Fold tabs on the two notched sides over toward center 1½ inches. Sew down 1⅜ inches from folded edges. Do all four tab sections. (See steps A and B.)

6. Cut Velcro strips into two 8-inch-long pieces. Pull strips open so you have four pieces.

7. Place Velcro strips along the four (9-inch) sides of the carrying mat. They should be ⅛ inch in from edges. Make sure tacky sides of Velcro face each other. Pin securely. (Fold the two edges that were left open at the side of the mat in ½ inch and pin). (See step C.) Sew ⅛ inch in from each Velcro edge to secure. (See step D.)

8. Cut dowel into two 12-inch pieces. Slip each piece into pockets at top of carrying mat.

9. Place the cup, spoon, and bib in the center of mat.

10. Tie toys to 18-inch lengths of ribbon. Tie the other end of ribbon to one of the dowel pieces. Now you can place toys into mat also.

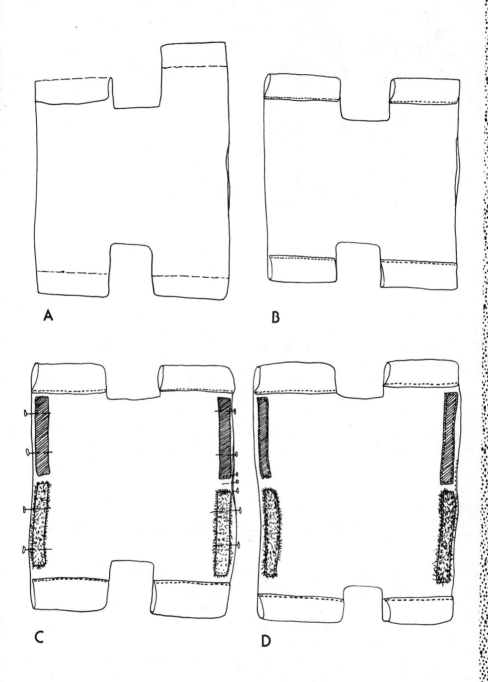

A

B

C

D

Chapter 5

Gifts for Preschoolers

The 3- to 6-year-olds are the great adapters. They start out concerned with their own little worlds and gradually learn to cooperate, share, and to please the adults with whom they interact. When you're thinking of gifts for preschoolers, remember they love both quiet, solitary play, and very active play that engages their imaginations and allows them to use their newly acquired muscle coordination. Consider combining a "pop" commercial play item with a thoughtful classic.

✎ Put-together Suggestions ✎

- A superhero with a set of blocks
- A doll "of the moment" in a wooden cradle
- A tape deck with the newest in tapes
- Cartoon character sheets or bath towels
- A school bag in the up-to-the-minute design with school supplies tucked inside
- T-shirts with "in" sayings, photos, or designs printed on them
- A jewelry box with pop pins and barrettes inside
- A tooth fairy pillow that you've personalized with a marking pen, felt letters
- Art supplies in a tote bag, lap desk, or with an easel

- An assortment of books in a book bag
- A photo album with your child's photos put in
- An assortment of magazines with a subscription to one of the child's choice
- A game with a set time for a future play date
- Puppets and a puppet theater
- Dolls or stuffed animals with clothes
- People, farm, and animal sets with blocks
- Musical instruments and a date for an at-home family concert
- Tools and scrap wood
- Dress-up clothes (your discards, costumes, or just an assortment of hats) in a box or trunk (could also include makeup, doctor's kits)
- Pajamas in a pj bag
- Shoes or funny (animal) bedroom slippers in a shoe bag
- Knapsack with a favorite snack wrapped up inside
- An umbrella in a plastic tote
- Tent/playhouse with inflatable furniture
- A walkie-talkie and a lesson in Morse code
- A cookie jar filled with child's favorite cookies
- Barrette holder and barrettes
- An overnight bag with underwear, socks, and a new toothbrush
- Sand toys, sun glasses, and beach towel in a pail
- Money in a purse, pocketbook, billfold, or piggy bank
- Child-sized table with chairs, stools, or benches
- A kitchen set—oven, sink, play dough, food, dishes, pots, pans, and refrigerator (look for chip-ins on this)
- A cardboard grocery store with empty food boxes, cash register, play money, grocery bags, shopping cart, and play food.
- A little baker's basket, filled with baking utensils, recipes, and ingredients.

Doll-in-a-Necklace

This "paper doll" is made of felt. Fabric clothing cut-outs stick right on—no need for tabs; and the necklace is a fabric pocket with a strap attached. Make it special by making the doll a look-alike for the child.

1 piece of 9 × 12 inch cardboard

1 piece of 9 × 12 inch tan felt

Small ball of yarn that matches the child's hair color

Permanent marker pens In brown and pink or acrylic paints in brown, pink, and white

Assorted cotton fabric scraps, at least 6 × 6 inches

1 piece of calico fabric 6 × 12 inches

1 piece of tiny checked gingham 6 × 12-inch fabric in a color coordinated to the calico.

24 inches of ¼-inch ribbon in color to match calico
Craft knife
White tacky glue
Needle and thread

How to Make Felt Doll

1. Trace and copy doll pattern on page 60 onto piece of cardboard.
2. Cut out the cardboard doll.
3. Trace outline of doll on tan felt. Cut out.
4. Glue felt figure to cardboard figure.
5. *To make hair:* Tie 12 pieces of yarn together in the middle. Braid down each side. Tie ends with another piece of yarn.
6. Glue yarn hair to sides and top of face on felt. Leave ends free.
7. Mark eyes and mouth and color in cheeks with marker pens or paints.
8. Cut cotton fabric scraps into dresses, shirts, shorts, and tops. (See patterns on page 61 for suggestions.)

How to Make Necklace Pocket

1. Place the calico and gingham fabrics right sides together.
2. Sew ¼ inch in from all edges. Leave a 2-inch opening on one side. Clip corners and turn right sides out. Slip stitch the opening closed.
3. Fold fabric so calico is on the inside and form is now 5½ × 6 inches. Sew across bottom fold and up side openings ¼ inch in from edges.
4. Turn pocket right side out.
5. Attach each end of ¼-inch ribbon to top corners of pocket with needle and thread.

Place felt doll and fabric clothes in pocket to give.

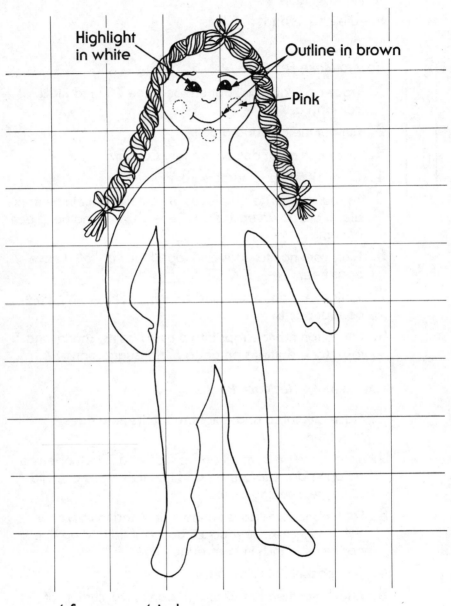

Highlight in white

Outline in brown

Pink

1 Square = 1 inch

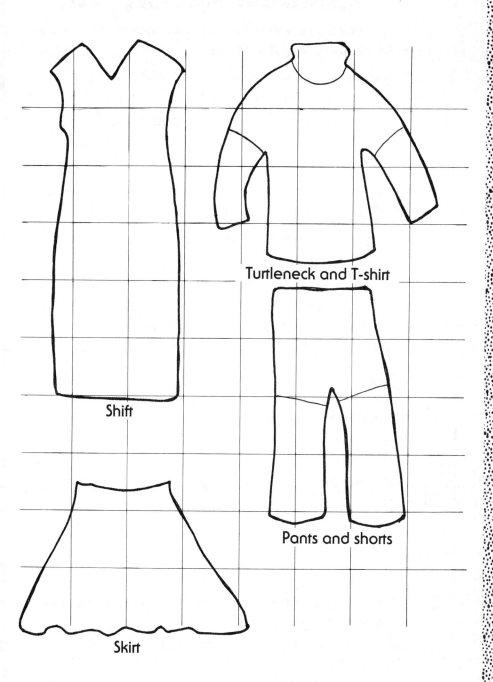

Turtleneck and T-shirt

Shift

Pants and shorts

Skirt

Handi-Pockets Apron

This pocket-style apron can carry woodworking tools, crayons, stuffed animals, cars for boys or girls.

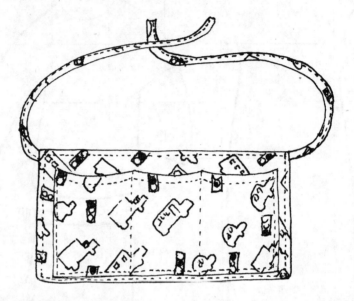

You Need

½ yard heavy-duty fabric (either 36 or 45 inches wide—cotton, broadcloth, canvas, duck)

Pinking shears (optional)

Pins

Iron

Toys and tools like those on pages 66–67 (optional)

You Do

1. Cut a piece of fabric 14 × 10 inches. (See cutting diagram, step A.)

2. Fold the two 10-inch sides and one 14-inch side in ½ inch and sew ⅜ inches in from edges. (See step B.)

3. Cut two strips of fabric each 2 × 18 inches to make two apron ties.

4. Fold each strip in half lengthwise. Fold both raw edges inward ¼ inch and press. (See step C.) Fold one end on each strip in ¼ inch and press. Now topstitch ⅛ inch in from folded edges to make apron ties. (See step D.)

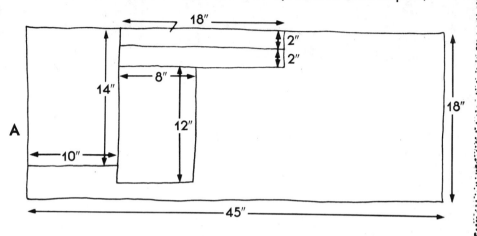

A

18″

2″

2″

14″

8″

18″

12″

10″

45″

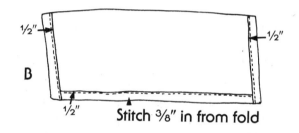

B

½″

½″

½″

Stitch ⅜″ in from fold

C

Topstitch ⅛″ in

D

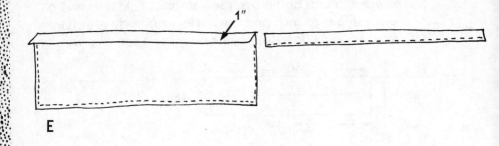

E

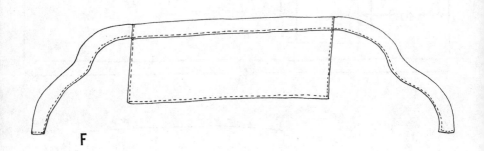

F

5. Fold the top edge (14 inches long) of apron down
1 inch. Insert 1-inch apron ties into top corners under the
folded section. (See step E.) Stitch across the top of
apron ¾ inch down from edge and across each tie end
to secure tightly. (See step F.)

6. Cut a piece of fabric 12 × 8 inches for pockets. Fold all
edges under ½ inch (see step G), and sew along one
12-inch side ⅜ inch down from edge. (See step H.)

7. Pin pocket piece to apron. It should be placed ½ inch in
from each edge and 1½ inch down from apron top.

8. Topstitch around three sides of pocket piece.

9. To further divide pocket, sew a line from top to bottom
4 inches from each side, creating three pockets: one
4 inches wide, one 3 inches wide, and the last 4 inches
wide. Reinforce each pocket section with another line of
stitching, directly over the first. (See step I.)

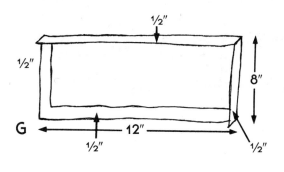

G

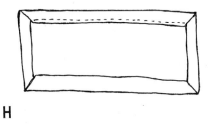

H

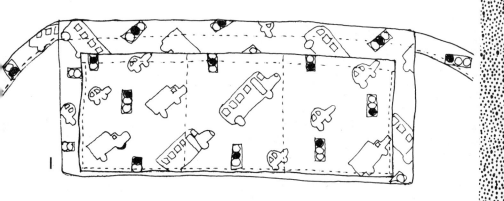

I

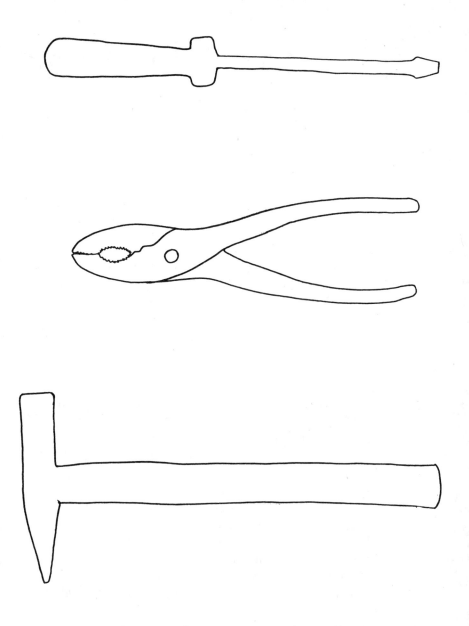

Chapter

Gifts for School-age Children

The 6- to 11-year-olds are the Great Doers who spend their leisure hours honing special physical skills; swimming, ball playing, skating, and using their hands. They are always busy, either active in games with friends or quietly building things on their own.

Gifts for young school-age children should encourage their confidence in their newly-emerging interests and talents.

⟡ Put-together Suggestions ⟡

- Sports equipment with two tickets to that sporting event or necessary accessories; for example, skateboard, knee and elbow pads, and helmet.
- A gift and a promise to spend time together: telescope plus a trip to a planetarium; backpack for camping; kites to fly together; packaged craft kit and a date to put it together; 14K gold earrings and a date to get ears pierced.
- Calendar marked with dates for movies, plays, concerts, or sporting events you will attend together in the coming months, marked in with the special love messages written throughout.
- Stethoscope and an anatomy book.
- Add-ons to existing collections.
- Fun makeup kit.

- Something to wear with unusual buttons or pins attached; a sweatshirt or T-shirt with bag of appliqués, glue, needle and thread, stencils and paints, or iron-on transfers.
- Art supplies in a school bag.
- Tool box with real tools, wood scraps, glue, and book of woodworking instructions.
- Make-your-own jewelry kit plus a jewelry box.
- Beach bag plus towel, sunglasses, lotion, and change purse with ice cream money.
- A bank book. Open a savings account for the child and make the first deposit.

Barrette and Jewelry Holder

Little girls love fancy barrettes, baubles, and beads. Here is a place to put that nice collection, where it can be seen and kept untangled and accessible.

Two 6-inch-diameter muslin-fabric circles

Fabric paint (can be acrylic—choose colors for eyes and cheeks that match the girl to whom you are giving this holder)

Fine-bristled brush (size 0)

4 to 6 ounces polyester stuffing

24 strands of 40-inch long yarn in color to match hair of girl to whom you are giving this holder

2 pieces of 8-inch-long ribbon

18 inches of 2-inch-wide lace

1 piece of ¾-inch-thick pine (approximately 14 × 9 inches)

Sandpaper

12-inch length of ¼-inch doweling
Wood glue (Elmer's)
2 sawtooth hangers
Tools: bandsaw or jigsaw, drill or drill press

1. Cut out pine, following diagram on page 72.
2. Sand pine smooth.
3. Drill ¼-inch wide holes in holder as shown in diagram. Each should be approximately ½ inch deep.
4. Cut doweling into 2½-inch segments. Add wood glue to tips and push into holes.
5. Add two sawtooth hangers in back.
6. Use fabric paints to paint face onto one muslin circle. (See diagram for placement of features.)
7. Place two circles right sides together and stitch ½ inch in from edges around top of head, leaving about 4 inches open. Clip curved seam and turn right side out.
8. Slip face over wooden circle.
9. Add some polyester fiberfill to puff out face side.
10. Slip stitch face on left and right sides, adding polyester fiberfill as you sew it closed.
11. Sew lace with a long basting stitch to gather to a 10-inch circle.
12. Sew lace collar around neck on face. Pull tightly to cover any raw edges left on muslin. Add a touch of glue to secure collar firmly to wood.
13. Tie the 24 strands of yard loosely in the middle and braid each side. Tie ends of braids with ribbon.
14. Sew braided yarn hair around edge of face. Braids should hang down.
15. Barrettes are placed on braids, jewelry hangs on dowel pegs.

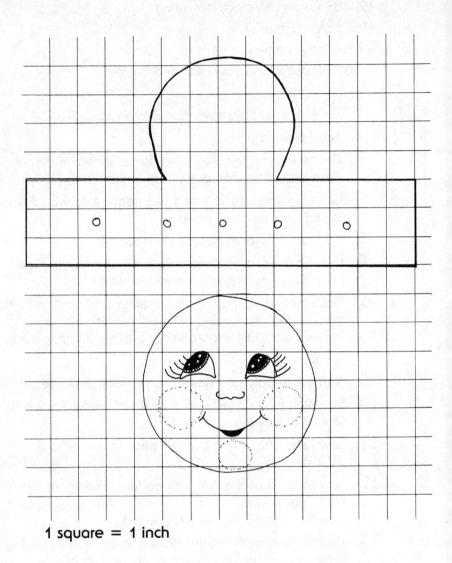

1 square = 1 inch

Birthday Box

Good things do come in small packages—24 of them, as a matter of fact! In this Birthday Box are 24 gift-wrapped packages. The box itself can be used later to hold collections of matchbox cars, rocks, shells, baseball cards, and so on.

One 24-section wooden soda box (check classified section of phone book under "Beverages" to find a bottling company where you can purchase box—and probably you'll have to buy the soda also)

2 eye screws (available in picture hanging kits with wire)

1 yard heavy wire

Choice of lettering:

—*red, white, and blue acrylic paints and "0" brush or*
—*alphabet soup noodles covered with polyurethane or*
—*carved letters available in some boutiques*

White (Elmer's) glue, if using noodles

White tacky glue, if using carved letters

24 gift items that you know the child would enjoy that can fit inside the box. Some suggestions are:

—matchbox or similar type of tiny metal car
—small box of interlocking blocks that make a vehicle (Lego)
—packages of bubble gum with baseball cards
—compass
—key ring
—key ring flashlight
—package of C or D batteries
—audio tape recorder cassettes
—unusual ball-point pen
—mini jigsaw puzzle
—yo-yo
—small rubber ball
—penknife

—whistle on a chain
—popular 4-inch high, movable figures
—markers
—paint box
—chalk
—marbles
—stickers
—photo of family or friends in a tiny plastic frame
—stick-up clock
—candy bar
—pad of paper

Ruler

Pencil

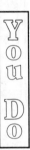

1. Measure and mark 2 inches down from top on either edge of back. Screw in an eye screw at both points.

2. String wire tightly between the eye screws. Twist wire ends tightly around the stretched wire.

3. Choose a way to letter the message:

   Happy Birthday All Year Long (greeting)
   Jason (child's name)
   May 3, 1978 (child's birthday)

   Glue alphabet soup noodles with wording to three center horizontal sections of box. Use Elmer's glue. Let dry thoroughly and cover with a coat of polyurethane (Zip-Guard).
   Paint in the greeting on horizontal sections with acrylics. Alternate colors on each word. Or:
   Use tacky glue to attach letters to top of box. Most letters are large so you may only be able to fit the child's name.

4. Wrap each gift separately and place one in each section. Wrap entire shelf.

Fun Pins

Here is a gift so simple, yet so much fun to create that your child might want to help you make it for friends. The pins can be worn on T-shirts, jackets, socks, or on bookbags.

1 package red oven-baked clay (Fimo or Sculpey III)

1 package blue oven-baked clay

1 package yellow oven-baked clay

4 pin backings (available in craft stores)

Hot glue stick gun

Rolling pin

Ruler

Sharp knife

White acrylic paint and brush

⅛-inch dowel piece (4 inches long)

1-inch section of Popsicle stick

2-inch piece of string

½-inch circle photo of friend

1. *To make balloon:* Roll a marble-sized piece of blue oven-baked clay into a ball. Taper one end to resemble a balloon. Bake acording to directions. Cool. Squirt a glob of hot glue on back side of balloon. Quickly set in piece of string and pin backing. Let cool and finish with dots of white acrylic paint. (Use tip of brush handle to make dots!)

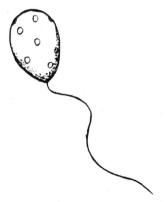

2. *To make the pinwheel:* Roll a half marble-size of oven-baked red and yellow clay together to make orange. Roll to ⅛-inch thickness. Cut a 1½ × 1½-inch square with a sharp knife. Make four diagonal cuts from each corner in toward center. Leave ¼ inch in center cut free. Pull each corner piece toward center to create pinwheel shape. Roll a pea-sized ball and press over corner points in center to secure tightly. Bake according to clay directions. Squirt a glob of hot glue on back side of pinwheel. Press in a pin backing and 2-inch piece of ⅛-inch doweling.

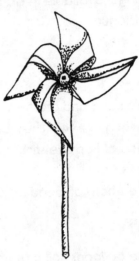

3. *To make the ice cream bar:* Blend a half marble-sized piece of red, blue, and yellow oven-baked clay into brown. Shape into a 1-inch long ice cream on a stick. Push the 1-inch section of Popsicle stick into the brown clay. Bake according to directions. Squirt a glob of hot glue on the back and press in pin backing.

4. *To make the all-day sucker:* Roll a half marble-sized red ball with a half marble-sized yellow ball into one 4-inch long snake. Roll only enough to mix colors slightly. Coil the snake flat. Push the ⅛-inch dowel into the coil and bake according to directions. Squirt a glob of hot glue on back side and press in the pin backing.

Variation: *Photo Pin:* Make a simple design pin shape such as the balloon. Cut a photo of a friend into a ½-inch circle size. Before balloon shape is baked, press the photo into the balloon to make an ⅛-inch indentation. *Remove photo.* Bake piece. Let cool thoroughly, then glue photo into indented spot. Experiment with other shapes and photos.

Canvas Game Rug

Any kid who loves playing on the floor will enjoy this attractive painted canvas rug.

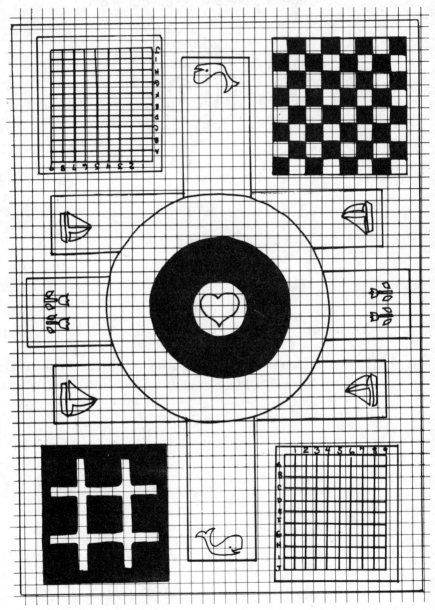

1 Square = 1 inch

1⅛ yards of 54-inch wide artist's canvas (finished on one side)

acrylic latex paint in the following colors: gold, colonial blue, barn red

alphabet stencil (available in stationery stores)

liquid polyurethane (Zip-Guard or Stencil-Ease's Stencil Kote)

yardstick

pencil

1-inch-wide paintbrush

masking tape

Aleene's tacky glue

1. Using the yardstick and diagram on facing page, measure and copy pattern onto canvas.

2. Follow color guide and paint each section. (Block off straight lines with masking tape to make painting easier.) Apply paint thinly.
   Basic background—gold
   Checkerboard—red on gold
   Tic tac toe—gold on red
   Battleship grids—blue on gold with red letters and numbers
   Heart—gold on blue circle on red circle
   Flowers—gold on red
   Boats and whales—gold on blue

3. Use a commercial alphabet stencil to make the letters, tracing them first and filling in with paint.

4. Let dry thoroughly for a day.

5. Fold all edges back 1 inch and glue down with tacky glue.

6. Brush on one coat of polyurethane over top side, completely covering the rug. Let dry for one day. Repeat with two more coats, letting each coat dry thoroughly. Paint two coats of polyurethane on the reverse side.

Game Rug Stencil Decorations

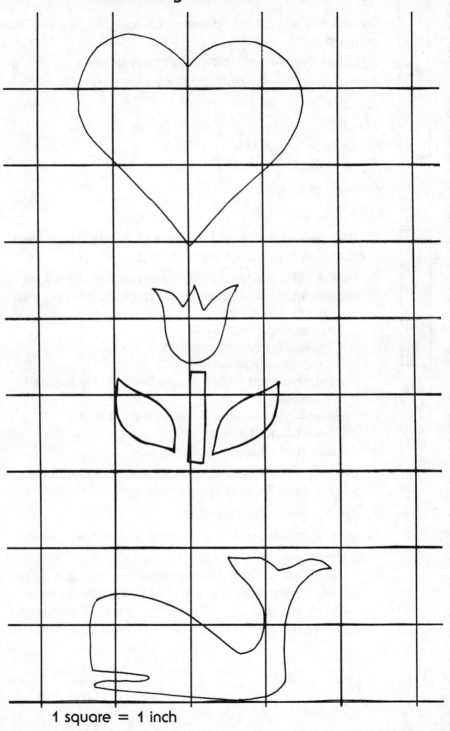

1 square = 1 inch

Money Ring

Give a bill of one, five, or ten dollar denomination as a ring that can actually be worn. Children can use it as a unique piece of jewelry (everyone will want to know how it's done) and even wear it to school (for emergency money) without losing it.

1-, 5-, or 10-dollar bill

Ring box

1. Place bill (so you can read all words) face down (green side up) on flat surface.
2. Fold white top border under (see step A on following page).
3. Fold bill in half lengthwise.
4. Tuck bottom half of bill under the folded border (see step B).
5. Fold entire bill in ½ lengthwise again.
6. Fold left side of bill upward about two-thirds of the way from the left side to make an L shape. Right angle corner on L will be a small diagonal fold (see step C).
7. Roll vertical part of L down and around finger toward back and up toward front so that it makes a circle with a 1-inch tab sticking up (see step D). Fold that 1-inch tab forward so that you will see the "1" of the one-dollar bill (see step E).
8. Fold horizontal leg of L to the left across front of circle under tab and through the circle. Let the tiny white border end fold forward over itself (see step F).

9. Fold vertical tab down and tuck its white border securely under the open space (see step F). You have a bill ring.

10. Roll both edges on round part of ring inward to create a tapered look.

11. Place "ring" in box.

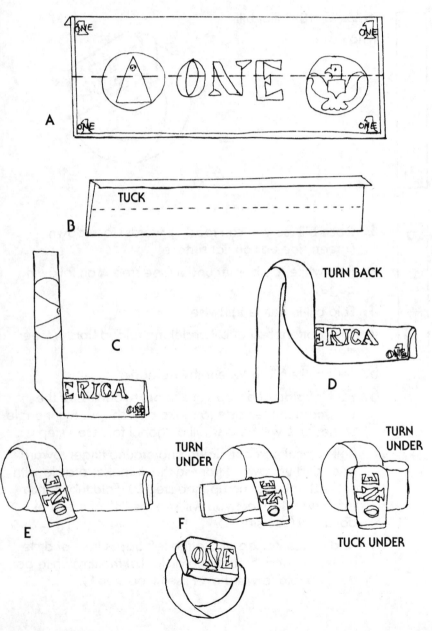

Chapter 7

Gifts for Teens

The 12- to 18-year-olds are the Great Pioneers—constantly breaking new ground in terms of what they *can* do and what they *may* do.

Adolescents are extremely conscious of their peer world. They are concerned about what they wear as being a sign of who they are. Their rooms are an extension of themselves and, consequently, very important.

So unless we know the adolescent well, gift giving can be a problem. To *really* impress them with a gift, we must know what sport, what team, what car, what rock group is their favorite. But even if we don't know all about this "Pioneer," we can give gifts that say "Here's something basic; you use it any way you want." These gifts enhance their search for freedom and their emerging adult skills.

Generally, they appreciate money and "grown-up" gifts, and it is usually the safe way to go. But remember that inside most teens, there is still a child saying, "I like to have fun and play." Don't be too surprised when a teen wants a doll (to "sit on my bed, of course") or a remote control Lamborghini to tear up cardboard ramps and career around chair legs!

The teen years contain some significant rites of passage that call for gifts which show the importance of the occasion. At these times consider giving gifts that will last a lifetime, such as: silver candlesticks, chalice, or passover dish for a bar/bat mitzvah; Bibles, crosses, prayer plaques, or framed religious pictures for confirmation; reference books, a set of luggage, fine jewelry, or a watch for graduation. You might also consider such special gifts as a coin collection or birth year coins, stock certificates, or bonds, bills in a wallet, or money clip.

ᐸᓍᑐ Put-together Suggestions ᓭᓯᔑ

- Scrapbook, diary, or photo album with recent photos inserted.
- A magazine in which you've pasted a picture of their face on an area of interest (e.g., in an outrageously expensive car, on a model in a gorgeous outfit), together with yearly subscription.
- A wastebasket that's been autographed by all his friends and family.
- Something to wear: accessories in a variety of colors—belts, socks, stockings in an organizer bag; night T-shirt autographed by family and friends.
- Shaving kit—mug, soap, and brush.
- Sports pennants and two tickets to a game.
- Lessons and an accessory for a favorite musical instrument, craft, or hobby (e.g., cooking lesson, cookbook, and casserole dish).
- Any car accessory (e.g., car visor) or use of the car on certain dates.
- Nail-care set and a date for a professional manicure.
- Photo of favorite actor/actress, rock star, or sports figure—autographed. (Write to their movie studio, team, TV or radio station. Note that this requires time.)
- Makeup kit and/or organizer with an assortment of lipsticks, eye shadows, mascara, and brushes.
- Money message poster—spell out a message with coins taped on a piece of cardboard for a poster or giant greeting card.
- Money tree—tie on paper bills (with ribbons or pipe cleaners) to a tree branch stuck into a pot/jar filled with sand or marbles.
- A composite picture frame with photos of the teen and best friends or family.

For the Student Off to School

- Monogrammed, personalized towels (so they will be less likely to lose them).
- A rubber stamp that says, "This book belongs to . . ." and stamp pad.
- An address/telephone book (with coins for calls taped inside) and stationery with stamped and addressed envelopes (to you).
- Cookies or favorite snack in tin, to be refilled on visits or through the mail. Or one box of goodies per month for months at school (from ten relatives).
- A framed photo of "the family" with little familiar reminders written around the mat border like: "Don't go to sleep too late!"
- Forget-Me-Not Kits in little plastic buckets (First Aid, Sewing, Grooming).
- When you are dropping a child off at school or visiting there, take a little extra time to explore the boarding school/college town for the following:

  A restaurant to arrange for a prepaid dinner for two.
  A theater to purchase two tickets to send in an envelope.
  A bake shop or pizza parlor that will deliver during exam time.

- Friendship quilt. Make (or buy) a quilt that has blank squares on which family and friends can write personal messages with permanent markers.

3-D Birthday Card

Here is *the* opportunity to say a lot of nice things about some-one in a gift that will become a permanent reminder of your love. It is a framed, handwritten story about the birthday person with miniature items depicting parts of the tale.

It is an irresistible gift on two accounts—the tiny objects draw one's eyes into the frame and the loving words, meant for just the one special person, keep them there.

An assortment of miniature items (see sample below)

A fancy frame (without glass) with a 10 × 14-inch opening

A piece of heavy, smooth illustration board

Craft knife

Ruler

Pencil

Felt-tip calligraphy marking pen

White tacky glue

Masking tape

1. Go to a shop that sells miniature items. It could be a dollhouse, craft, or toy store. Pick out the appropriate items for the birthday person; for example, favorite foods, sporting equipment, occupational and/or school paraphernalia, and hobbies.

2. Write a story about the person, mentioning these items directly. You can put it into a letter form such as "Dear————, or in a tale form such as "Once upon a time," or use a journalistic style: "Janice Doe is a fantastic student . . ." We have chosen a letter form.

3. Use the craft knife and ruler to cut a piece of illustration board to 10½ × 14½ inches.

4. Use pencil and ruler to lightly mark lines every ½ inch across the board from left to right. (You can choose to hold the board either horizontally or vertically.)

5. Write your message with the felt-tipped calligraphy pen held at a diagonal angle. (See calligraphic alphabet on pages 88–89.)

6. Leave space in your writing where you have a mini-item and glue it onto the board next to the words describing it.

7. Let ink and glue dry thoroughly in a flat position.

8. Place finished message picture in frame. Use masking tape around edges to hold in place.

ABCDEF
GHIJKL
MNOPQR
STUVW
XYZ

abcdefg
hijklmn
opqrstuv
wxyz

T-shirt Pillow

What do you do with a loved-but-outgrown T-shirt that your child refuses to get rid of? Make it into a pillow, of course.

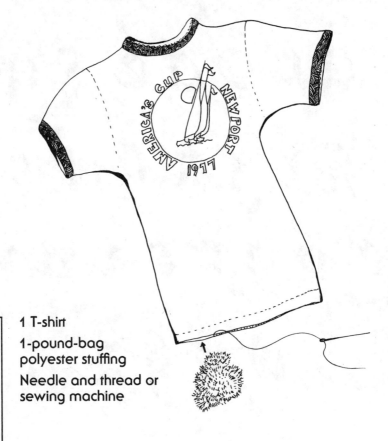

You Need

1 T-shirt

1-pound-bag polyester stuffing

Needle and thread or sewing machine

You Do

1. Topstitch the neck opening closed.

2. Topstitch the arm opening closed.

3. Stuff the T-shirt with polyester stuffing.

4. Topstitch the bottom of the T-shirt closed.

Personalized Nightshirts

An extra large-sized T-shirt presents ample opportunity to make it special with names, games, and designs. You can personalize it for birthday, holiday, or cheer-up gifts. Teens will enjoy wearing one as a nightshirt or beach cover up.

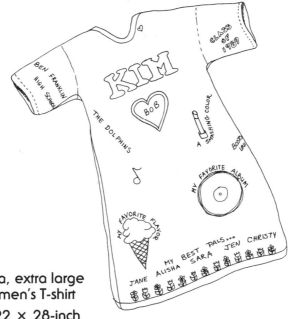

1 extra, extra large (XXL) men's T-shirt

One 22 × 28-inch piece of poster board

Permanent marking pens in your choice of colors (use Sharpie or Deco Color Opaque Paint Markers)

Pencil

Scissors

1. Pull T-shirt over poster board so it is stretched slightly.

2. Use pens to draw names, games, or designs on the shirt. Hold fabric tightly and use a sketching stroke with the pen.

3. Above are a few illustrated samples of things you can put on T-shirts.

Chapter 8

Gifts for Adults

An adult is a very complex combination of tastes, interests, likes, dislikes, prejudices, and longings.

On my thirty-eighth birthday, for instance, I was a little late coming home from work, and as I walked into the house, there was my husband dressed in a tuxedo with a rose in one hand and a glass of wine in the other. He had prepared dinner just for the two of us. After the initial shock of seeing him so out of character, I realized that he knew how ambivalent I had been about approaching middle age. After dinner, he gave me a totally impractical, sexy nightgown, an antique ring he had found in a junk store, and a miniature Queen Anne's chair for my dollhouse. He indulged my fantasies, not with an expensive gift such as a parcel of land or original artwork which we couldn't afford, but with fun and through surprises.

～c Put-together Suggestions ～

Traditional Gifts with a Twist

- A bouquet of flowers for their birth month.
- Chocolate message (see page 204).
- A piece of jewelry with the birthstone. For a mother or grandmother include the birthstone of all the children and grandchildren.

Flowers for Birth Months

BIRTH MONTH	FLOWER
January	Carnation
February	Violet
March	Jonquil
April	Sweet Pea
May	Lily of the Valley
June	Rose
July	Larkspur
August	Gladiolus
September	Aster
October	Calendula
November	Crysanthemum
December	Narcissus

- A bottle of vintage wine with a wineglass on which you've written a special message with an indelible marker.
- A record, tape, or sheet music of a song popular during their birth year.
- An "At Home Scavenger Hunt"—hide small gifts around their house that can be found by following written clues.

Gifts to Indulge a Fantasy

- A year's subscription to a state lottery.
- A psychic or astrological reading or visit to a hypnotist.
- Instead of giving one rose, plant a rose garden.
- A string quartet or professional singer/entertainer hired for an evening. Local music schools provide an excellent, relatively inexpensive talent source.
- A mini-trip or vacation (even a day at a spa will do)—mark an X on a detailed map and let her have the surprise of finding the place.
- An artist's sketch of their house, children, pets. Contact a local art school and bring along photos for the artist to use.

Birthstones

Wearing birthstones is said to bring good luck and influence personality.

MONTH	STONE	MEANING
January	Garnet	Constancy
February	Amethyst	Sincerity
March	Aquamarine	Courage
April	Diamond	Innocence
May	Emerald	Love and success
June	Pearl	Health
July	Ruby	Contentment
August	Sardonyx	Married happiness
September	Sapphire	Clear thinking
October	Opal	Hope
November	Topaz	Fidelity
December	Turquoise	Prosperity

- A luncheon with a favorite local author, columnist, or someone your friend admires. Call the publisher or paper and ask. If it works out, arrange for expenses in advance.
- Make a wish come true. Give lessons and/or equipment in something they've been wanting to do (e.g., scuba diving).
- Buy shares of a $2.00 stock. It could skyrocket.
- A facial or body massage, or a body massage kit in a basket (scrubbing brush, foot and back roller, body oils, etc.).

Gifts of Time

- Teach someone how to do something. For example, give a lesson in crocheting (with needles and yarn); in cooking (with utensils, book, or ingredients); in music (singing, piano, guitar, recorder with music book); in calligraphy (with pens).
- Be a helpmate: a chauffeur for the day; waitress or bartender at a party; or cook on-call when needed.
- Take photographs of the person for an individual portrait or one of their whole family; make a photo album of photos taken at the person's party; videotape a special event (e.g., an ice skating competition).

- Share-a-gift: a museum membership (plan a trip together), or tickets to the ballet, opera, or a sporting event.

"Number" Gifts

- A dozen eggs—11 originals and 1 fancy hand-crafted egg or egg-shaped paperweight with a note: "You're unique."
- A quantity appropriate to the occasion. For a fortieth birthday —forty of anything, 40 carrots (You're a 40-carrot person), 40 fifty cent pieces, 40 chocolate kisses.

Gifts from the Group

Pool resources with family members and friends to coordinate giving one of these at a party, luncheon, or dinner.

- A gift-a-month for a year —assign one month to each person and set delivery time the same for each month, and give a bouquet of flowers; a favorite baked item, or a fine bottle of wine; a gift certificate to 12 different restaurants. The birthday person will be reminded of your caring and of this party for the next 12 months.
- An overnight bag filled with wrapped toiletries, fancy night wear, and underclothing. Each guest adds something to the bag.
- Exercise equipment. Include a mat, tape, record, or video-tape and/or certificate for a class.
- Add accessories to one gift (e.g., a camera plus lens attach-ment).
- A vacation for a week. Each guest pays for one day. Present this in travel log book where each guest writes a message.
- A "Memory Lane Book." Purchase or make a scrap album. Ask everyone to write a letter to the person. Begin each letter with, "Since I've known you . . ." or "Remember when . . ." Also ask each person to bring or send a photo of the person and caption it.
- An antique charm necklace (or silver or gold charm holder and chain) for which everyone gives a different charm.

Beach Mat

No ordinary towel will suffice for the true sun and sand worshiper. This mat rolls compactly, yet has pockets to stash keys, sunglasses, or suntan lotion. A padded, built-in pillow adds comfort for the head. Omit the pillow and you have a handy exercise mat!

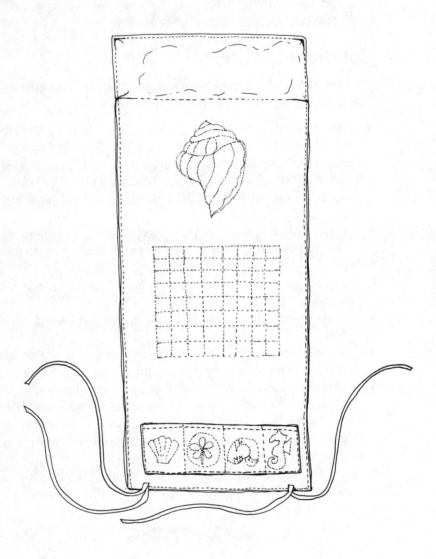

4¼ yards striped canvas cloth (36 inches wide) or 2 yards of solid 54-inch wide canvas. If you choose to use this fabric, follow the directions, but please note that your beach mat will be only 54 inches long rather than 72 inches, and you must use other scrap fabric pieces to make the pockets.

1 piece of 36 × 72-inch quilt batting (thick). Use polyester if available.

12 ounces polyester stuffing

2 yards of grosgrain ribbon (color coordinated to striped cloth)

Tape measure

Pins

Iron

1. Measure and cut striped canvas cloth into two pieces, each 36 inches wide × 72 inches long. (See step A.) Small remnant will be used for pockets.

2. Place right sides together on flat surface. Cover with the 36 × 72 inch piece of polyester quilt batting. Pin all around edges. (See step B on following page.)

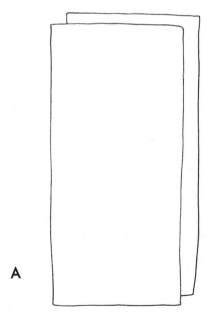

A

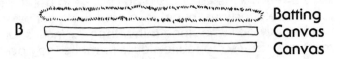

B   Batting
Canvas
Canvas

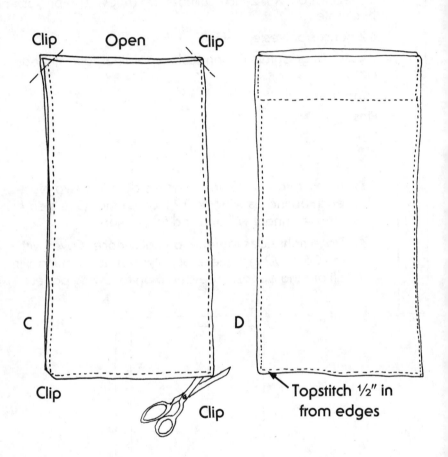

Clip   Open   Clip

C

Clip

Clip

D

Topstitch ½" in
from edges

3. Turn whole piece to canvas side and stitch ½ inch in from edges around the two long sides (72 inches) and one short side (36 inches). Leave one short side open to turn right side out after clipping the corners. (See step C.)

4. With right sides out and quilt batting inside, run a machine topstitch ½ inch in from the three edges that are already sewn. (See step D.) This will hold the batting more firmly as well as be more attractive.

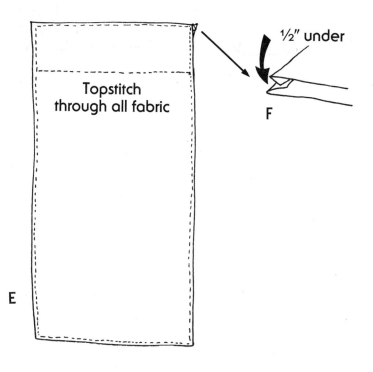

½" under

Topstitch
through all fabric

F

E

5. Topstitch a line 12 inches across, parallel to and down from the open end. (See step E.) This creates the "pillow" section. Stuff lightly but firmly with polyester stuffing.

6. Close the remaining opened end. Fold each edge in ½ inch and slip stitch closed. Topstitch ½ inch in from closed end. (See step F.)

7. Cut fabric remnant to size 9 × 24 inches. Turn all edges under ½ inch and press down. Sew ⅜ inch in from one long (24-inch) edge to make pocket top. (See step G.)

8. Pin pocket in place on "foot" end of beach mat. Place pocket 3 inches up from short edge and 6 inches in from either long edge. Topstitch through all fabrics, ⅜ inch in from folded pocket edges along the sides and bottom. Sew one line of stitching in pockets every 5¾ inches to divide the one pocket into four smaller ones. (See step H.)

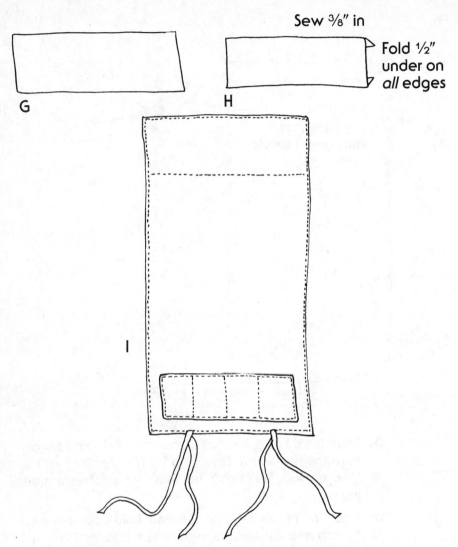

Sew ⅜″ in

Fold ½″
under on
all edges

G

H

I

9. Cut ribbon in half to make two pieces, each 1 yard long. Fold each piece in half. Place one piece of folded ribbon 3 inches in from outer corners on each side of the "foot" of beach mat. Pin ribbon on already sewn (½ inch in from edge) line on the same side of mat where pockets are located. Machine sew each ribbon securely on the crease. Ribbon ends will be loose. (See step I).

10. *To roll beach mat.* Start from "pillow" side and roll tightly toward "foot" end. Pockets should be facing outward. Tie roll by dividing ribbons and wrapping each part around the roll and end with a bow.

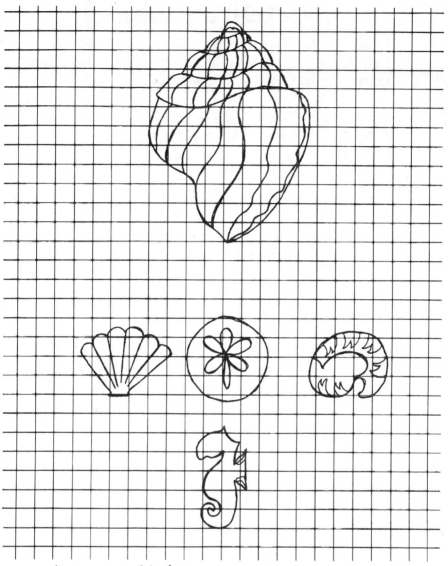

1 square = 1 inch

Copy design from book onto completed beach mat
and machine stitch outlines through all fabrics.

Celebrity Money

Wish someone "Happy Birthday" and "Good Luck" for the coming year with this funny money. It has the birthday person's face on it in place of Abe's or George's.

1 photo of the person's face
Photocopies of the photo
Paper bill in any denomination
Transparent tape
Craft knife

1. Make black and white photocopies of the person's face.
2. Cut out each copy of face around hairline and collar with a craft knife.
3. Roll a loop of transparent tape and place behind photo of birthday person.
4. Press photo over the face on the bill.
5. Repeat for as many bills as you'd like to give.

Relaxation Sandbox

Sand is a natural relaxer. Make this tiny sandbox with its miniature sand castle as a conversation piece to sit atop a busy person's desk. This sandbox can have a calming, relaxing effect on anyone who plays with the tiny shovel, filling up the tiny pail with sand.

1 finished hinged wooden box (approximately 6 × 5 inches) available in craft or gift stores (we've also used wooden cigar boxes for a more rustic look)

½ cup sand (plus about 2 more cups for the sandbox)

¼ cup cornstarch

⅓ cup water

Plastic wrap

Miniature items: shovel, pail, sea gull (available in dollhouse store)

Tiny seashells

Toothpick

1. *To make sand clay:* Mix ½ cup of sand with cornstarch in a saucepan. Slowly add water and cook. Stir constantly until mixture thickens into a consistency like mashed potatoes. Cool and cover with plastic wrap.

2. Mold a walnut-sized piece of sand clay into a cube to resemble a castle. Use a toothpick to hollow out a door, windows, and squared-off battlements around the top of it. Mold a long wall to place around the castle. Let dry (preferably in the sun) for 24 hours.

3. *To assemble the sandbox:* Place remaining sand in it, set up castle and walls. Add the shovel, pail, and sea gull. Sprinkle a few tiny shells around.

A Life in Miniature

Put all the things someone especially loves in a tiny setting to make this gift. Each "Life in Miniature" is a highly individualized sculpture. Each setting is one-of-a-kind.

1 piece of ¾-inch pine approximately 14 × 14 inches

1-inch-long paneling nails

1 miniature table or desk

1 miniature chair

Miniature items to hang on the back wall (interest related)

Miniature items to place on the table (interest related)

Alphabet soup noodles

Acrylic or latex paints

1-inch-wide paintbrush

Elmer's wood glue (or Aleene's "Tacky")
Ruler
Sandpaper
Hammer
Sawtooth hanger

1. Measure and cut a piece of wood 8 × 6 inches. Sand and set aside.

2. Cut a rounded-edge (6 inches long × 3 inches wide) shelf. Sand and glue to bottom edge of 8 × 6 inch piece to form an L-shaped shelf and background. Nail (from back) to reinforce shelf.

3. Paint in desired colors. Let dry thoroughly.

4. Glue miniature items to back "wall."

5. Use a tiny (1 inch wide × 2 inches long) piece of scrap wood (could be a furring strip or thin piece of pine) to make a shelf. Glue on "wall." Place books or objects on shelf.

6. Glue miniature table and chair onto "floor" area.

7. Place miniature objects on table and glue down.

8. Use the alphabet noodles to personalize the sculpture (e.g., "Harry's Hide-Away" or the alphabet over the teacher's chalkboard).

Variations: When cutting backgrounds, make the "wall" piece of pine into a schoolhouse shape for a teacher. It could be a church shape for a minister or a store shape for a storekeeper. Vary the woods, too. For example, a nautical setting is best done on pieces of driftwood. A den setting looks great with stained rather than painted wood.

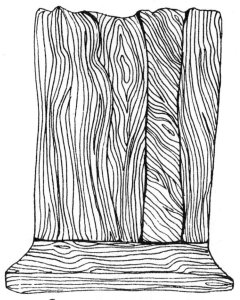

Grainy gray driftwood

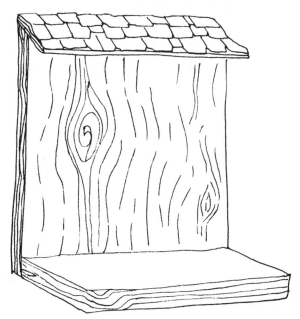

Stained pine and shingle storefront

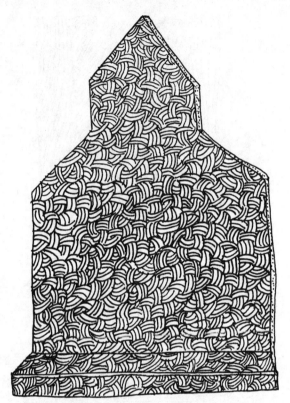

Dull red painted schoolhouse

Family Tree Pillow

Any mom, grandmother, or favorite aunt will appreciate this pillow. Each member of the immediate family is represented by a heart on the tree. Place children close to their parents.

You Need

2 waxed stencil papers
Craft knife
Ball-point pen
Stencil paint in green, pink, brown, blue, and white
Masking tape
Stencil brush #6
A pointed fine (0) brush
1½ yards good-quality muslin
18-inch square piece of quilt batting
Cotton quilting thread (beige)
Needle

¼ yard pink solid fabric
¼ yard pink calico
Sewing machine with beige thread
12-ounce bag polyester stuffing

1. Trace family tree (see pattern) onto stencil paper. Use only the number of hearts you will need. You can add hearts by moving the stencil paper around and tracing the same hearts over again until you have desired number. Remember to place children close to their parents. Grandchildren are placed outward on the tree but near their parents.

2. Cut out design with craft knife.

3. Place stencil on center of 16-inch square piece of muslin. Tape in place.

4. Stencil tree first with brown paint. Let dry.

5. Stencil hearts next with pink paint. Place masking tape over leaves that are close to hearts. Let dry.

6. Tape edges of hearts on stencil that are close to leaves, and stencil leaves green. Let dry thoroughly.

7. Use the fine-pointed brush and the blue paint to write the names of family members on each heart.

8. When dry, iron on reverse side.

9. Place the piece of quilt batting behind the stenciled fabric. Place a 16-inch square piece of muslin behind the batting.

10. Use cotton thread and needle to quilt, through all three layers (muslin, batting, muslin), around the outline of each heart and tree trunk (see step A).

11. Cut solid-colored pink fabric into four strips:

   two are 2 inches wide × 16 inches long
   two are 2 inches wide × 18 inches long

12. Sew the two 2 inch wide × 16 inch long strips to the sides of pillow. Sew the two 2 inch wide × 18 inch long strips to the top and bottom. Use ½-inch seams.

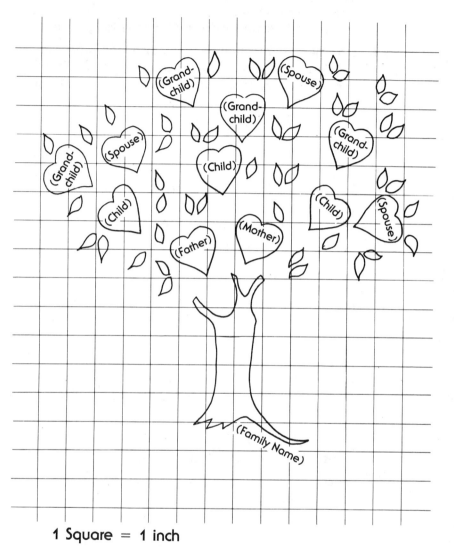

1 Square = 1 inch

13. Cut muslin into four strips:
    two are 2 inches wide × 21 inches long
    (top and bottom)
    two are 2 inches wide × 19 inches long (sides)

14. Sew the two 2 inch wide × 19 inch long pieces to the sides next to the pink calico. Sew the two 2 inch wide × 21 inch long pieces to the top and bottom.

15. Cut pink calico fabric into four strips:

    two are 2 × 22 inches
    two are 2 × 24 inches

16. Sew the two 2 × 22 inch strips to the sides of pillow. Sew the two 2 × 24 inch strips to the top and bottom. The pink and muslin solids and calico fabric form a "frame" around the pillow. (See step A.)

17. Cut a 22 × 24 inch square of muslin for the back of the pillow.

18. Place right sides together and machine sew ½ inch from edges all around. Leave 5 inches open to turn pillow right side out. Clip tips off each corner before turning.

19. Sew a line of machine topstitching around pillow (except for 5-inch opening) at junction of pink solid and muslin strips. (See step B.) Sew with beige thread on muslin.

20. Stuff pillow with polyester stuffing.

21. Slip stitch closed the 5-inch opening.

22. Machine stitch the 5-inch unsewn border between the pink strip and muslin strip.

Sewing the Strips

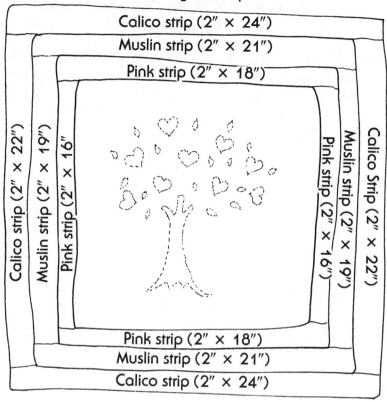

Calico strip (2" × 24")
Muslin strip (2" × 21")
Pink strip (2" × 18")

Calico strip (2" × 22")
Muslin strip (2" × 19")
Pink strip (2" × 16")

Calico Strip (2" × 22")
Muslin strip (2" × 19")
Pink strip (2" × 16")

Pink strip (2" × 18")
Muslin strip (2" × 21")
Calico strip (2" × 24")

A

Topstitching on Finished Pillow

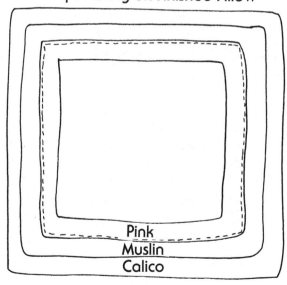

Pink
Muslin
Calico

B

Gingham Cross-Stitch Sampler

Sometimes the best gift ideas come from the receivers themselves. Flo, a waitress on the TV show *Alice,* had a pet saying, "Kiss my grits." It's hers and it is unique. If you were to give Flo a gift, what would she get more of a kick out of than a "sampler" you've made with her favorite saying done in old-fashioned cross-stitch?

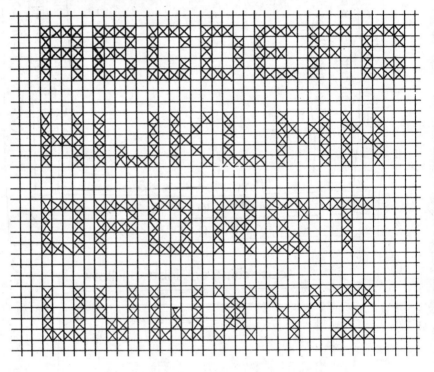

½ yard light-colored (yellow, light blue, pink, lilac, or light green) gingham. It can be either the ⅛-inch or ¹⁄₁₆-inch (approximate size) squares, depending on how long the saying is or how large you want the words to be

Graph paper (8 squares to an inch is close to ⅛-inch gingham)

Pencil

Embroidery hoop

6-strand embroidery thread in a dark color. Some nice combinations are:

—*brown on yellow gingham*
—*red on blue gingham*
—*purple on lilac*
—*dark green on light green*
—*rose and green on pink*

Embroidery needle

Stretcher frame in your choice of size (available in art and framing stores)

Staple gun

Masking tape

Sheet of white poster board

1. Sketch out your saying on graph paper. Check alphabet diagram on page 114 to form letters. Make each letter on graph paper using *x*'s.

2. Cut a piece of gingham to fit stretcher frame plus 2 inches all around.

3. Count the squares from the top and sides and pencil in the saying, using *x*'s for each letter.

4. Place designed gingham piece in embroidery hoop.

5. Work cross-stitch in four strands for ⅛-inch size checks and in two strands for ¹⁄₁₆-inch size checks.

6. When completed, stretch gingham over stretcher frames and tape in place. Use staple gun to secure fabric to wood. Make sure you staple over the tape to prevent fabric from fraying.

7. Cut a piece of white poster board to exact size of the back opening made by the stretcher frame. Slip it behind the cross-stitching to enhance the design. Use masking tape to secure it to the stretcher frame.

8. Frame as desired or leave as is.

While-You-Wait Kit

How many times have you found yourself sitting in a car, waiting to pick up someone and becoming more annoyed each minute because you knew you were wasting valuable time that you could be spending elsewhere?

Here is the perfect gift for anyone who plays the "waiting game." It provides the raw materials so that you can spend time making lists, writing letters and reminders, reading, cleaning the car, and even filing and polishing your nails!

You Need

½ yard heavy cotton or lightweight canvaslike cloth

½ yard of print to coordinate with the solid-color cloth

1⅔ yards of ⅛-inch-wide ribbon

1 piece of corrugated cardboard (10½ inches by 8 inches)

Ruler

Pins

Tacky glue (optional)

Items to put into kit:

> *stationary and envelopes*
> *postage stamps*
> *pens*
> *nail file and polish*
> *pocket book of short stories, inspirational sayings or jokes*
> *rag*
> *garbage bag*
> *list of ways to relax*

1. Measure and cut a piece of the print fabric to 24 inches × 18 inches.

2. Place print fabric face down on surface and place a piece of 24 inch × 18 inch solid-color fabric (good side up) on top. All edges should meet. (See step A.)

3. Fold both fabrics up ½ inch around edges. Sew about ¼ inch in from edges on three sides. (See step B.)

4. Take corrugated cardboard and slip it between the fabrics so it is 2 inches from edge of left side (18-inch side) of fabrics and approximately 3¼ inches from top and 3¼ inches from bottom of fabric edges. Hold firmly in place and sew through both fabrics with foot of sewing machine right against the cardboard. You will encase the cardboard in fabric. (You may wish to glue cardboard in place before you sew to make it easier. However, the glue may pucker the fabric and the result is not as nice.)

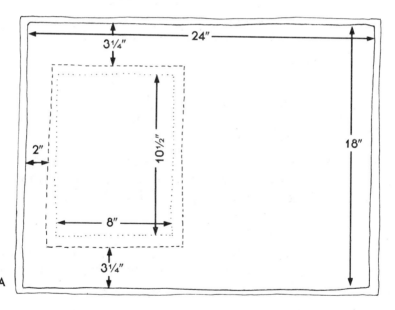

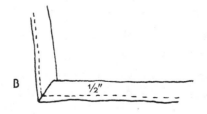

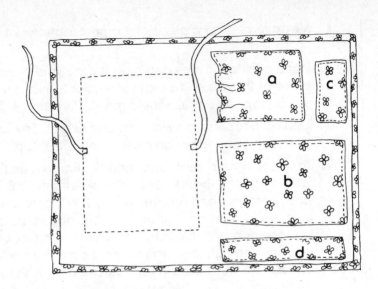

5. Sew up fourth edge of folded fabrics.

6. Now fold all edges another ½ inch up so raw edges are concealed. Pin the folded edges in place. Sew ¼ inch in from edges all around.

7. Cut "pocket" pieces from the calico for the kit:

   pocket a: 7½ inches × 7 inches
   pocket b: 8 inches × 12 inches
   pocket c: 3 inches × 5 inches
   pocket d: 3 inches × 12 inches

8. Turn all pocket-piece edges under ½ inch and stitch ¼ inch in from folded edges. Sew a basting sitch along one 7½ inside of *pocket a.* Gather slightly to make a puffy pocket.

9. Position pockets as shown above. Pin in place. When in place, pocket *a* measures 5 inches × 6 inches. Make adjustments in the gathers to fit that space if necessary.

10. Sew all pockets down on three sides.

11. Cut ⅛ inch ribbon into two 12-inch pieces and one 36-inch piece.

12. Sew one end of a 12-inch piece to either side of the encased cardboard.

13. Fold top and bottom inward. Fold sides up and tie with remaining ⅛-inch ribbon to hold.

Treasure Hunt

Here is a unique birthday party idea sure to please even the person who already has everything. Invite friends and relatives to purchase one gift each in different stores in one small shopping center, or Main Street. For example, one friend might purchase a belt from the clothing store, another stationery in the bookstore. Each gift is to be paid for, wrapped at the store, and *left there*—with the person's name on it, of course, and gift card enclosed.

The lucky person is given printed instructions to go from store to store to pick up the gifts. (If you're lucky, the store employees will even sing "Happy Birthday.") The last instruction will be to go to a restaurant in the same area, where everyone waits for a surprise lunch or dinner!

Arrange for the treasure hunt to start at the store furthest away from the restaurant. (Have the birthday person pick up his or her own birthday cake at a bakery, or arrange to have one at the restaurant.) Enjoy watching the person open gifts over lunch or dinner!

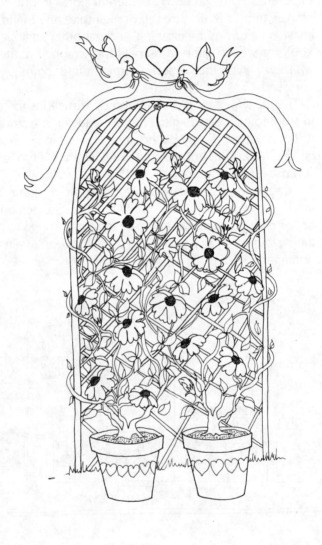

Chapter 9

Wedding Gifts

With the announcement of a wedding come several opportunities to shower a couple with many gifts.

An engagement gift says, "Congratulations," and often is a kindness to the parents of the couple as much as to the couple themselves. We suggest a small romantic gift, because there are showers and a wedding ahead. Too large a gift early on will put you into a predicament later. Make the engagement gift a book of love poems, an art book about "love," an ornate frame for their engagement photo. You can jokingly send your congratulations with a money ring (see directions on page 81) and a note saying, "You might have the real thing on your finger, but now you'll need more of this kind."

ᥱᑐᵣ᷑ Put-together Suggestions ᥬᢂᠵ

For the Shower or Engagement Party

- **Favorite Recipe**
  Ask everyone coming to the shower to bring a copy of his or her favorite recipe written on a 5 × 8 size card. Make sure each contributor signs his or her name. Decorate a large-size index file box with decals or stickers. Paint the bride's and groom's name in enamel paint on the cover of the box. At the shower

121

have everyone present the recipe card. You might want to have everyone actually bring the favorite dish along (as a potluck luncheon) with the recipe, but this is optional.

- **Photograph the party.**

Use an instant camera and place all the photos in an album you've brought. Let everyone add written comments on slips of paper to add with the photos.

- **Message Apron**

Use permanent markers (DecoColor) to add personal thoughts to a canvas or duck cloth apron. Here's a message we like:

A recipe for A Successful Marriage: Take two people, add a heap of love, an overflowing cup of humor, a dash of patience, a pinch of tolerance, heavily spice with sex, and season with wisdom. Mix well.

Have everyone sign their names.

- **Silk Flower Arrangement**

Ask all the guests to bring a silk flower to the shower. You should suggest colors and varieties. Bring a wonderful vase or basket fitted with floral foam and dried or silk fillers. (Ask the florist to help you do this if you can't do it yourself.) Let everyone place her flower in the arrangement. Upon doing so, mention what each flower stands for and what you wish for the new couple. When completed the bride will have not only a home decoration but a lovely remembrance of family and friends from her shower.

- **A Honeymoon Salad (a gift of money)**

Here is a fun gift, which actually turns out to be a great gift of money.

Fill a lovely wooden salad bowl with bills in your choice of denominations. Cover with plastic wrap, tie with a ribbon, make a bow, and attach a salad spoon and fork server. With a marker, write on the label, "A honeymoon salad: Lettuce alone without dressing" and include with bowl.

et the Flowers Speak for You!

FLOWER	WHAT IT SIGNIFIES
Red rose	Love for each other
White rose	Serenity
Violet	Loyalty
Lily of the valley	Happiness always
White daisy	Innocence
Ivy	Fidelity
Tulip	Love from us
Pansy	Thinking of you
Orchids	Beauty
Lily	Purity
Gardenia	All-pervading love
Blue forget-me-nots	True love always
Daffodil	Best regards
Jasmine	Sensual pleasure

Unity candles = Wedding celebration

For the Wedding

A wedding gift is an absolute *must.* Even if you don't plan to attend, you must send a gift. A wedding gift is more than the material object. It reflects your wish for love, happiness, health, and a long life together.

Useful is the key word for gifts for the couple just starting out. A telephone call to the parents can tell you which appliance, tableware, linens, furniture, silverware, crystal, or china the couple might need or appreciate most, and which stores they are registered in. Wedding gifts are more expensive than most gifts. Make yours even a little more special.

● Fill a picnic basket with wedding reception goodies (e.g., two slices of wedding cake, two glasses, a bottle of champagne, napkins, other nibbles and flowers). Give to the couple before they leave so that later that night they can have their own party. Add some spending money for the honeymoon.

- Something silver: Ingots in a personal vault or the key to a safety deposit box in which you've put the ingots. Contact a local bank for how to arrange this (the couple's signatures will be required); a frame for their wedding photo or with one you've taken and enlarged; an ice bucket with champagne and silver goblets.
- A cappuccino coffee machine with two special mugs on which you've written a personal message with indelible ink.
- A gas grill with barbeque utensils in the pockets of his and her chef aprons.
- A coffee machine that grinds and brews coffee and an assortment of exotic beans.
- A pasta maker with red checked tablecloth and napkins, pasta bowls, and forks.
- A clam steamer or lobster pot with a certificate for two lobsters.
- An ice-cream maker with scoop; glass dishes for sundaes and splits and all the trimmings.
- A small refrigerator (for the bedroom perhaps) stocked with wine, cheese, and breakfast nibbles.
- An electric smokehouse and a gift certificate to a local fish store.
- Soup tureen, with soup crocks, spoons, and your favorite recipes slipped into each bowl.
- An inexpensive parcel of land in a remote area. It could one day turn into a very valuable possession.
- A bicycle built for two with a basket of picnic goodies (and helmets). Check with secondhand shops.
- A case of investment wine for the year of their marriage. It could mature into a winning vintage year.
- A videotape of their wedding ceremony. Rent the equipment if you don't have your own.
- A loan of your vacation home, camper, or boat for a few days. The couple might even choose to use it for the honeymoon. Be sure to stock the refrigerator with wonderful food for the couple to enjoy.
- Welcome the honeymoon couple home with either:

A fabulous gourmet-style meal prepared and delivered to the couple's home. Place in containers in their refrigerator and leave a note on the door.

Fill the couple's refrigerator with the basic foods—milk, eggs, condiments, breads, juices, frozen meats. Tie a giant bow around the whole refrigerator.

- If your talents include one of these, offer your services as:

    A flower arranger for the bride and groom. (Pick and purchase the fresh or silk flowers.)

    A seamstress to help with bridal and attendants' gowns.

    A chauffeur for the wedding day. Bring the bride to have her hair done. Drive the couple to and from the wedding. Drive the couple to the airport.

    A reupholsterer. Have the couple's separate pieces of furniture reupholstered to blend well together. (This is a particularly good gift for the second-time-around couple.)

- A Chinese wedding feast or other special dinner out for the couple is a great gift to be used after all the wedding-honeymoon hullabaloo has died down. Make arrangements with the restaurant and give a handwritten gift coupon on parchment scroll (with instructions to call in advance to set the date and time, because many of the dishes require several days' preparation). All arrangements for these special dishes are made and prepaid well in advance. The restaurant will expect them.

- Tuck money (or money substitute) inside a book:

    An antique book—which will help them choose and purchase their own antique.

    An art book—for a piece of artwork.

    A guidebook (on restaurants, resorts, and country inns) for that meal or weekend stay.

    A how-to book on gambling for the couple honeymooning at a gambling resort.

    A stock market book—with a gift of shares of stock. The dividends will be a constant reminder of your present.

    A gourmet cookbook with a certificate for cooking lessons at the local gourmet shop.

Birdseed Buds

Almost every bride and groom plan some little memento to be given to the wedding guests as a remembrance of their day. Usually these are matchbooks, napkins, or candy favors. Here is a lovely idea for someone to make for the bride and groom to give out right after the ceremony; satin "rose buds" filled with birdseed. The roses open so the birdseeds can be flung out to shower the bride and groom as they leave the chapel for their reception or honeymoon. The advantage of using birdseed is that there is no need to sweep up afterward as when using rice, which if left can be harmful to birds, or confetti. The birds do the cleanup! The satin roses may be closed to regain their bud shape so the guests can take them home.

½ yard satinlike fabric, 45 inches wide. This will make 54 buds.

2 rolls green floral tape

1 package heavy florist's wire

Needle and thread

Birdseed

1. Cut fabric into 54 pieces each 3 × 5 inches.

2. Fold in half with right sides together (piece is now 3 × 2½ inches) and sew ¼ inch in from raw edges along the 3-inch side. (See step A.) Turn right side out.

3. Gather one side along the 2½-inch edge and place one piece of heavy wire on it about ½ inch up.

4. Wrap gathered portion with green floral tape, pulling it tightly to make it very secure. (See step B.)

5. Continue to wrap entire wire "stem" with floral tape.

6. Open bud at top and fill with 1 tablespoon birdseed. (See step C.)

7. Fold and crimp top edge of bud down securely to contain birdseed. (See step D.)

8. Wrap the buds and give with a note:

"Use these buds at your wedding. They will delight your guests and surely make the birds sing songs of joy for you both!"

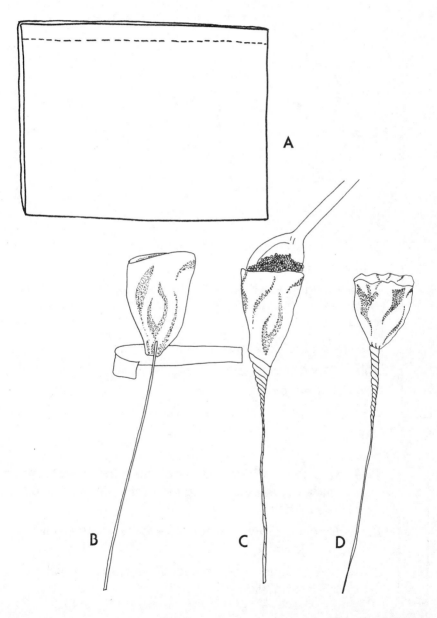

A

B   C   D

Personality Pillows

Embroider portraits of a couple, one on each pillow.

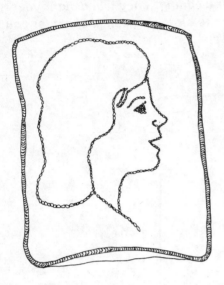
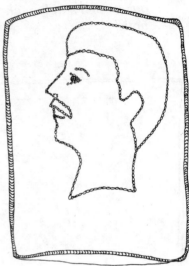

One 35 mm slide of the person's face

Slide projector

⅔ yard beige to tan-colored 45-inch-wide fabric (good muslin, polished cotton, or cotton/polyester)

Pencil

4 skeins embroidery thread in brown

Embroidery needle

3 yards brown piping

One 12-ounce bag polyester stuffing

Pins

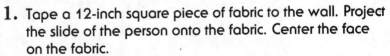

1. Tape a 12-inch square piece of fabric to the wall. Project the slide of the person onto the fabric. Center the face on the fabric.

2. With pencil, draw in all facial features. Include hair, glasses, jewelry.

3. Repeat technique on another 12-inch square with another facial slide.

4. Use an outline embroidery stitch to sew around all the lines you've drawn. Use six strands for hair area. Use four strands for facial features.

5. Cut two more 12-inch square pieces of fabric for pillow backings.

6. Pin brown piping ½ inch in from raw edges on embroidered pieces.

7. Place backing over right side of embroidered piece. Pin in place.

8. Sew ½ inch in from edges all around pillow. Leave 5 inches on one side open to turn pillow right side out. Clip tips off corners. Turn pillow and stuff. Slip stitch closed.

Picnic Basket Set

A picnic basket set for two makes a romantic statement. Combine it with a wedding-guest signed tablecloth and you have a most memorable gift. Here's how to make a lovely 45 × 48 inch tablecloth.

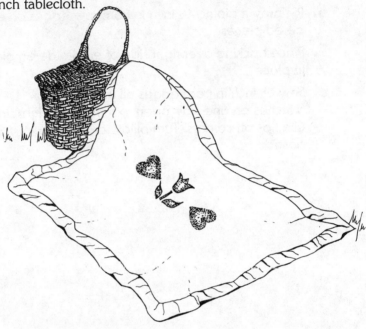

You Need

2⅓ yards 45-inch wide muslin and 1 more yard cut into inch-wide 45-inch-long strips

2 sheets of plain paper

Ruler

Waxed stencil paper (almost transparent)

Masking tape

Craft knife

Stencil paints

Medium-sized stencil brush

Needle and thread

Scissors

Permanent marking pen

Sewing machine (optional)

1. Prepare muslin by washing, drying, and pressing the wrinkles out of it. Cut the muslin into 2 pieces. One piece is 1⅓ yards and the other is one yard.

2. Draw the tulip and heart pattern on paper, using the diagram on page 133.

3. Place 1 sheet of stencil paper over each drawing and tape in place. Place on several thicknesses of newspaper.

4. With a sharp craft knife, cut on outlines of pattern as you see it through the transparent waxed stencil paper. You will keep the whole paper and discard the interior pieces. Remember, you want good, clean lines. If by chance you cut into the stencil paper at a corner, you must tape the cut on both sides of the paper so your paint will not "bleed" there.

5. Place your stencil in center of 1⅓ yard piece of muslin. (Measure 24 inches in from each side and 22½ inches in from top and bottom to locate center.)

6. Tape stencil and muslin to hard surface covered with four layers of newspaper.

7. Set up brush with small amount of paint on bristles. Tap excess paint on scrap paper.

8. Stencil design one color at a time by tapping the brush straight up and down, working from the outer edge of the stencil to the center. Traditionally a stenciled pattern is darkest at the edges and leaves some background color showing through in the center.

9. Repeat with another color. Use masking tape to cover already colored parts of the stencil design that might be too close to where you will be stenciling.

10. Let dry. Iron on reverse side.

How to Make Ruffled Border

1. Cut six strips: each is 6 inches wide by 45 inches long from the remaining one-yard piece of muslin. Sew the strips together end to end, with ¼-inch seams, to make one continuous strip 267½ inches long (or 22¼ feet).

2. Fold long strip in half so piece is 3 × 267½ inches or 22¼ feet. Use a basting stitch to sew in from raw edges

about ¼ inch. Do the basting in four sections, each about 5 feet long.

3. Carefully pull one basting thread to gather the long strip into a ruffle. Pull from each end until the 5-foot-long ruffle fits one of the 45-inch sides of the stenciled piece of muslin. With right sides together, pin ruffle to tablecloth piece. Continue basting, pulling the thread to make a ruffle, pinning to cloth until all four sides are done.

4. Machine sew the ruffle to the cloth about ½ inch from all raw edges. Trim edges with scissors. Use a machine zig-zag stitch along edges to finish and add strength. Press on right side.

At the wedding reception, set out the cloth on a hard, paper-covered surface and ask each guest to sign it with the perma-nent marker (preferably color coordinated) and add their wishes for the newly married couple. Add the date under your stenciled design.

To complete the picnic set, combine the cloth with

A small-sized picnic basket—one with a cover is nice

2 plates and glasses or cups (glass or tin is preferable)

2 sets of utensils

A couple of small covered serving bowls

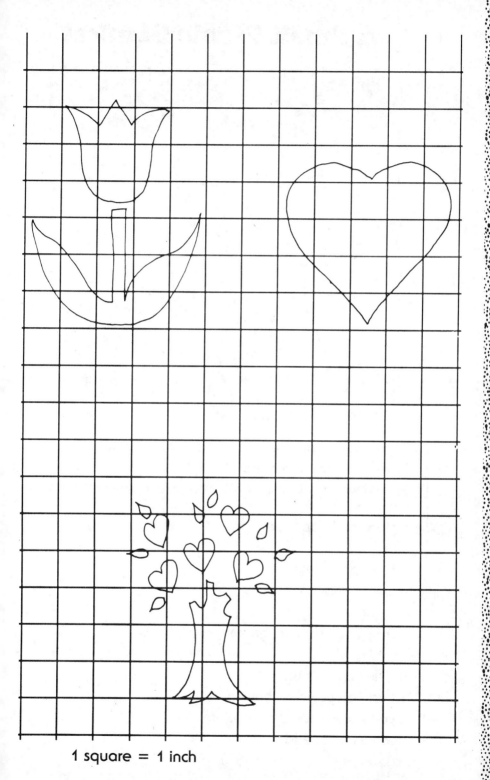

1 square = 1 inch

A Small Picnic Blanket

2 yards solid-color cotton (or cotton/polyester blend)

¾ yard coordinated calico

¾ yard white or muslin (whichever goes better with first two items listed)

1 piece of sandpaper

Ruler

Plain paper (3 sheets)

Waxed stencil paper

Masking tape

Stencil paints (brown, green, pink)

Stencil brush

Fine-liner paintbrush

1 package polyester batting

3 yards coordinated color ⅛" ribbon

Needle and thread

Scissors

1. Prepare all the fabric by washing and drying.

2. Measure an 8-inch square with ruler on sandpaper. Cut it out carefully.

3. Use this sandpaper square as a pattern to trace and cut out and set aside:

   12 solid-color squares
   12 calico squares
   12 muslin or white squares.

4. Draw the heart, tulip, and tree patterns with five small hearts on paper using the diagram on page 133.

5. Place a sheet of waxed stencil paper over the heart pattern and tape in place. Place on several thicknesses of newspaper.

6. With a sharp craft knife, cut on outline of pattern as you see it through the transparent stencil paper. Remove centerpieces.

7. Repeat above procedure with tree pattern and tulips.

8. Cut only enough small hearts to have one for each member in family.

9. Use the white or muslin pieces for the stenciled work. Place your heart or tulip pattern on center of muslin or white square (measure in 4 inches from each side).

10. Tape stencil and muslin to hard surface covered with four layers of newspaper.

11. Stencil using brush, with small amount of paint, with an up and down tapping motion. Work from the outer edges of the stencil, where the paint is darkest, to the center, where it barely covers fabric.

12. Continue to stencil six hearts and four tulips in all.

13. Stencil two trees on remaining 2 muslin or white squares. Use brown for the trunk and green for the leaves.

14. When trees are completely dry, stencil correct amount of small hearts in blank spaces between leaves.

15. Let dry and iron on reverse side.

To Assemble Quilt:

1. Sew squares together in strips from left to right as follows: (*important—leave only ½"-inch seams and be exact!)

> row 1—tulip, calico, solid, heart, calico, solid
> row 2—solid, tree, calico, solid, tulip, calico
> row 3—calico, solid, heart, calico, solid, heart
> row 4—heart, calico, solid, heart, calico, solid
> row 5—solid, tulip, calico, solid, tree, calico
> row 6—calico, solid, heart, calico, solid, tulip

2. Sew rows together, placing row 2 below row one and row three below row 2 etc.

3. With fine liner paint brush and stencil paint draw in family names under each tree and bride and groom names under center hearts.

4. Cut a piece of solid colored cotton to fit assembled squares (43 inches × 43 inches).

5. Cut a piece of 45-inch × 45-inch polyester batting.

6. Place assembled squares face up on a hard surface. Place solid-colored cotton right side face down on squares. Place batting on top of all. Pin around all four edges about 2 inches apart.

7. Machine sew all three layers. Sew on backside of assembled squares. Use ½-inch seams. Leave 8 inches unsewn to turn quilt right side out.

8. Turn quilt and slip stitch closed.

9. Make 13 small bows with 8 inches of ⅛-inch ribbon. Use a needle and thread to sew them on quilt as shown in picture. Sew directly through all the layers of quilt.

His and Hers Chef's Aprons

Here's a humorous gift that keeps on giving.

Fine-tipped (DecoColor) permanent marker pens in your choice of colors

Favorite recipes of the receivers

2 heavy, light-colored duck, canvas, or denim aprons

Write his favorite recipe on the front of his apron and her favorite recipe on hers. When one is a noncooking spouse, you can write in a recipe for boiling water or you can give step-by-step directions for ordering fast foods from the local take-out restaurant.

Pressed Wedding Flowers and Invitation

An invitation or an announcement has special meaning for the couple. You can give a lovely gift after the wedding which incorporates their invitation and flowers from the wedding celebration. A few flowers can be gathered from the guest tables or the place where the ceremony was held. If you are able to obtain one special flower from the bridal bouquet, all the better. The flowers are pressed, mounted around the invitation, and framed.

Fresh flowers, greenery. Vary the sizes and colors. Try to pick flowers that are not too thick—roses, daisies, stephanotis, baby carnations, baby's breath are fine.

Wedding invitation or announcement

A book to press flowers in—an old telephone book is perfect

A piece of mounting or mat board about 2 inches larger than the invitation or sized to fit a commercial frame (8 × 10 or 10 × 14 inches)

¾-inch white or beige lace (enough to go around the paper edge of the invitation)

Ruler

White tacky glue

Homemade pouncer (directions follow) made with a pencil, cotton ball, rubber band, and 1-inch square piece of cotton cloth

Waxed paper

½ yard of ⅛-inch wide white or beige satin ribbon

A frame with a glass in it

1. Begin pressing flowers as soon as possible. Place one flower on a page. Make sure that petals are spread open and leaves are spread out.

2. Place a pile of books on top to increase weight.

3. Leave in place for two weeks.

4. Make a pouncer to apply glue. Roll the cotton ball between your fingers until it is compressed and fits tightly into the 1-inch square of cotton cloth. Pull up the edges and attach the balled piece of cloth to the eraser end of a pencil with the rubber band.

5. Assemble the framed-flower invitation:

   (a.) Mount the invitation to the mat board with small dabs of glue. Use a ruler to center it. Cut lace pieces to fit around the edge of invitation. Dab with small amounts of glue. Glue into place to overlap edges. Place a clean sheet of waxed paper over it and press with a stack of books until dry.

(b.) Arrange the dried flowers around the invitation, placing them at diagonal corners or just along bottom or flowing down from the top.

Some arrangement ideas are:
(c.) When the flowers are in place, turn over one at a time and dab with the pouncer which has been dipped in slightly watered-down glue. Flip over into place and continue gluing down each flower, leaf, and stem. Make tiny bows of ⅛-inch ribbon.
(d.) Let dry for several hours. Gently place board with flowers and invitation under glass into frame.

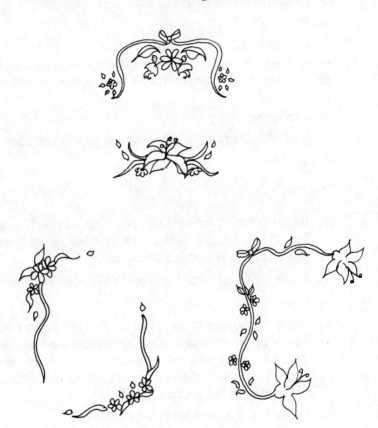

Nest Egg

The birds do it . . . the bees do it . . . so why don't we do it? Make a nest egg, that is! Help launch a newly married couple with one gift that always fits, is the right color, and never needs to be returned—money. Cash or a check given inside a beautiful wedding card is always appropriate. To make it special and unforgettable put it in a nest egg in a basket.

A shallow (8 × 10-inch approximately) open basket with a tall handle

2 × 4-inch piece of green florist's Styrofoam

Floral wire

Handful of Spanish moss

White silk flowers—3 lilies or 3 gladiolus

15 floral picks

Green floral tape

5 pastel silk rose buds

2 stems of silk ivy

A small bunch of white stardust or snowflake (bleached baby's breath)

2 yards of 1¼-inch white satin ribbon

1 large pastel or silver plastic egg in which stockings are sold

Hot glue gun

Fine shredded excelsior or pastel Easter basket grass

Wire cutter

1. Set basket in front of you. Determine the highest center point of the handle, then place the piece of Styrofoam one quarter of the way down the left side of the handle. Use floral wire wrapped around it and twist it tightly to secure in place. Secure further with hot glue under foam onto handle.

2. Loosely stretch and cover the Styrofoam with Spanish moss.

3. Use wire cutters to clip the long stems from the lilies (or gladiolus), leaving about 1 inch next to the flower. Wrap the wires on the floral picks around the short stem and cover with green floral tape. Place tape near flower and twirl stem as you stretch tape around wires, stem, and top of pick.

4. Continue to clip stems, then wire each piece and wrap with tape. Do the same for the stardust or snowflake flowers by holding a small bunch in one hand and wrapping it.

5. Poke large flowers into Styrofoam first, then add the two ivy stems. Next add the rose buds and finally the bunches of starlite. (See illustration above for placement of items.)

6. Make a bow about 5 inches in diameter with the satin ribbon. Use floral wire to secure the loops in the middle. Wire on a pick and tape wires. Insert into Styrofoam to the left of lilies.

7. Place bills of your choice inside egg. Place excelsior in basket. Set egg in middle of grass.

Chapter 10

Anniversary Gifts

Cinderella and Prince Charming, Snow White and her Prince —all lived happily *ever* after, or so the fairy tales often ended. Real life is *not* the stuff of which fairy tales are made. Given all the ups and downs of married life, the fact that we have any anniversaries at all to celebrate makes each one special. Many couples, particularly in the early years of marriage, enjoy private celebrations. But as the marriage matures, couples enjoy the fuss made by family and friends who take them to dinner or share an anniversary cake and champagne. And the marriage partners will want to put a little extra care into the gifts they give each other.

Put-together Suggestions

- An adult education course—sign them up for something new such as ballroom dancing, foreign languages, and prepay for the course.
- Hire a limousine for an evening (it could be a student willing to dress up as a chauffeur in his own car!). Include a bottle of wine.
- A romantic weekend at a country or bed-and-breakfast inn. (Get all the kids to chip in on this. There *are* affordable places.)

145

- A restaurant guidebook with a gift certificate to one of those listed.
- Slip money into two lovely tin or wooden "mad money" boxes labeled "his" and "hers."
- Two lobsters with crackers, butter, and butter crocks.
- A catered meal at home complete with candles and music. Make it an aphrodisiac dinner by including an oyster appetizer, asparagus as a vegetable, and figs for dessert.
- A year-long gift of 12 dinners out—one for each month from 12 friends or relatives in 12 different restaurants or their homes. Keep the date the same each month. If the anniversary is October 22, make the dinners on November 22, December 22, and take their photo at each dinner. At their next anniversary present them with a book of menu/recipes and photographs.
- An offer to videotape or photograph their party. Present the photos in a special album.
- A painted portrait of the couple and/or their children. Check with a local art school or gallery for names of artists.
- Couple/parent wedding photos in a triple frame. Obtain a photo of the couple at the time of their wedding and of each of their parents' wedding pictures. Place the couple's photo in the center frame and flank with each parent's picture.)

We tend to remember the tenth, fifteenth, twentieth, twenty-fifth, thirtieth, fortieth, or for those lucky few, the fiftieth-year anniversary with a splashy party. These anniversary years call for an appropriate gift to commemorate the couple, as well as the party. If we like, we can stick with the gifts that have traditionally been associated with these milestone years.

Traditional Gifts

- 10—Tin, Aluminum—antique tin filled with special candy or cookies; candlestick holders; country or primitive tinwork; cookie cutters, picnic tinware plates and cups, punched tin lantern; a carton of aluminum foil; cake tin and cake.
- 15—Crystal—glassware, champagne glasses (and champagne), dinner bells, handblown or cut pitchers, sculptures (my husband loved a 3-dolphin sculpture); watches, chandelier, mobiles, jewelry (hearts), rock candy, crystal ball, geodes (rock and crystal formations.)

- 20—China—pots de creme sets with a fabulous recipe, commemorative plates, dishware, porcelain statues, tea sets (and teas), antique vases, bone china cups (each with a different pattern), antique porcelain-faced dolls, salt and pepper shakers, Chinese kite, fortune cookies on Chinese cookie plate, china vase with 20 flowers in it.
- 25—Silver—tableware, candlesticks, a homemade fruitcake reminiscent of their wedding cake on a silver platter with a silver cake knife, silver jewelry, a charm holder and appropriate charms, or a bracelet and charms representing events with dates engraved during the past 25 years, a silver tie clasp (and tie) for him, a silver pin for her; silver coffee and tea service, silver ingots, silver dollar from their marriage year, silver coins spelling out a message.
- 30—Pearl—pearl jewelry—one pearl for each year of marriage, a box with inlaid mother-of-pearl, a mother-of-pearl handle on a pocketknife, fresh oysters with perhaps a lovely shell-shaped china platter to put them on; an article of clothing made or knitted with pearl button trims.
- 40—Ruby—jewelry, red glassware—hand-blown goblets (check out a crafts gallery); ruby red day lily plants for the garden.
- 50—Gold—black stationery with luminous gold marker; gold jewelry such as chains, lockets, pocket watches, or knives; a gold charm holder and some charms that represent the couple; gold coins (Krugerrands); gold-rimmed china (Lenox); gold-leaf picture frame for a photo of the whole family; a bowl of goldfish.

Salad Garden for Two

This tiny garden in a barrel is great for the country couple or the wish-we-were country couple. It is particularly well received by the older couple who may find it hard to grow their own.

½ barrel or wooden keg (available in garden shops)

Hand or electric drill

Large bags of potting soil (garden shop will advise the number depending upon the size barrel you choose)

Small bag of peat moss

Fertilizer (manure or Miracle-Gro)

Rocks

Seedling plants (1 cherry tomato, 2 cucumbers, 1 basil, 1 parsley, 2 garlic, 2 lettuce)

1. With the drill, drill five holes (approximately ¼–⅜ inch wide) in the bottom of the barrel for drainage.

2. Bring the rest of the ingredients for this salad garden to the couple's home. Let them determine where it will go.

3. Place a layer of rocks on the bottom of the barrel.

4. Pour in soil and mix with a few handfuls of peat moss.

5. Add fertilizer according to package directions.

6. Place plants in barrel and water.

Note: You may want to take on the responsibility of fertilizing the plants every few weeks.

Clothespin Personalities

A miniature clothespin person brings character to so many gifts. The clothespin personality uses a real facial photo of your special person and creates a unique figure that can be used on desks, in plants, on shelves, on soft sculptures, as ornaments, or anywhere that someone would love to see themselves. Make one clothespin of the wife and one clothespin of the husband.

For Female

Fabric scrap 15 × 5 inches

A peg-type clothespin

2 cotton balls or same size polyester

1 round toothpick

Close-up photo of woman's face (must fit on top part of clothespin)

Yarn scraps for hair (match yarn color to hair color)

Needle and thread

White tacky glue

Ruler

1. *To make bodice:* From the 15 × 5-inch piece measure and cut a piece of fabric 2 × 1 inch. (See step A on following page.)

2. Glue around clothespin about ½ inch down from round top. (see step B.)

3. *To make skirt:* Measure and cut a strip of fabric 12 × 5 inches. (See step A.) Sew a basting stitch along one long edge about ½ inch in. Pull threads to gather skirt at waist. Sew ends of fabric strip together to make back seam of skirt.

4. Turn skirt inside out and place upside down on clothespin so gathered waist is over the approximate waist position on clothespin and skirt is covering the round head part and slightly overlapping bottom of bodice (See step C). Glue into place and wrap a long piece of thread around gathered fabric to hold tightly. Now turn skirt right side out. You will have a bouffant-style skirt.

5. *To make sleeves:* Cut two pieces of fabric, each 1½ × 3 inches long. (See step A.)

6. Fold all raw edges under ⅛ inch and glue down. Sew a basting stitch along both 3-inch long sides. Before you pull the basting threads, sew the two 1½-inch wide sides together to form seam about ⅛ inch in from edges of inverted fabric.

7. Turn fabric right side out. Place one cotton ball inside. Pull both sets of basting threads tightly to form a puffy sleeve. (See step D.) Tie threads securely. Clip excess.

8. Break toothpick in half. Add a dab of glue to broken end and insert almost all the way into tiny hole formed by gathered fabric on one end of sleeve.

9. Dab a large amount of glue to the other end of sleeve and stick in place on clothespin.

10. Repeat steps 6 through 9 for other sleeve.

11. *To finish doll:* Cut out photo around face and glue onto clothespin on front, rounded, top part.

12. Cut yarn to match hairstyle. For example, if person has long hair, glue on long strands of yarn. Short curly hair calls for coils of yarn glued all over wooden head. Make yarn hair overlap top and side edges of photo to conceal it. (See step E.)

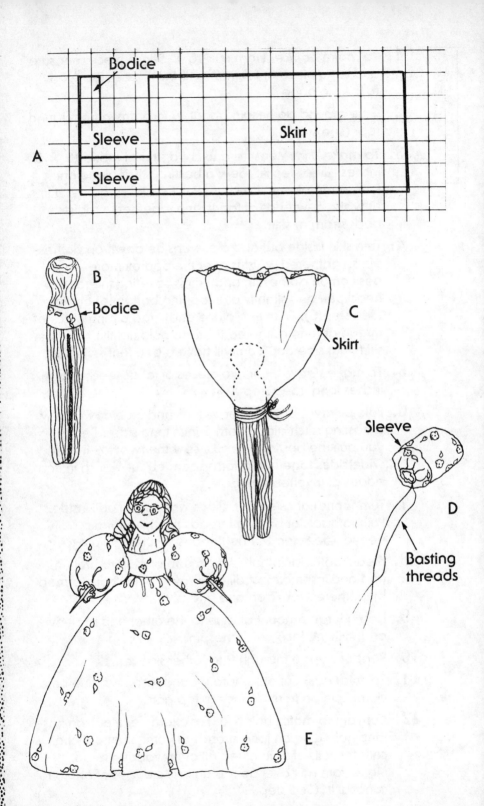

A

Bodice

Sleeve

Sleeve

Skirt

B

Bodice

C

Skirt

D

Sleeve

Basting
threads

E

For Male

1 piece of dark blue felt approximately 9 × 12 inches

1 peg-type clothespin

Blue thread and needle

1 round toothpick

Close-up photo of man's face (must fit on top part of clothespin)

Yarn scraps for hair (match yarn color to hair color)

Glue

Ruler

Black broad-tipped marker

1. *To make trousers:* Cut two pieces of felt, each 2½ inches square. (See step A.)
2. Glue square piece of felt around each leg on clothespin. (See step B.)
3. *To make jacket:* Cut out blue felt jacket using jacket pattern shown in step C.
4. Glue underpart of sleeves together to form rounded sleeves.

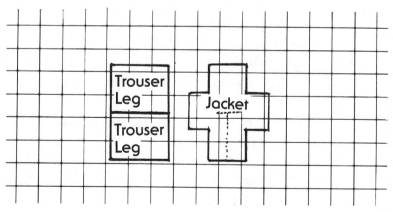

A

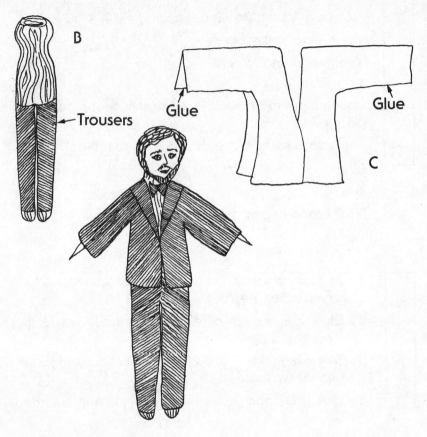

B

Trousers

Glue

Glue

C

5. Glue side seams of jacket.

6. Use blue thread to tack back a lapel on each side of front of jacket.

7. Break toothpick in half. Dab broken end with glue and insert into sleeve so only point shows. Repeat for other arm.

8. Glue coat onto clothespin. Overlap jacket front and glue together.

9. *To finish doll:* Cut a scrap (⅛ × 2 inches) of blue felt and gently tie a tiny bow. Trim ends. Glue in place under chin area as a bow tie.

10. Glue on cut-out facial photo.

11. Cut and glue on yarn scraps for hair (see step #12 in female figure section).

12. Color in foot tips of clothespin with black marker.

Family Silhouettes

Here is a wonderful gift for a family-oriented couple. Make a framed silhouette of each of their children.

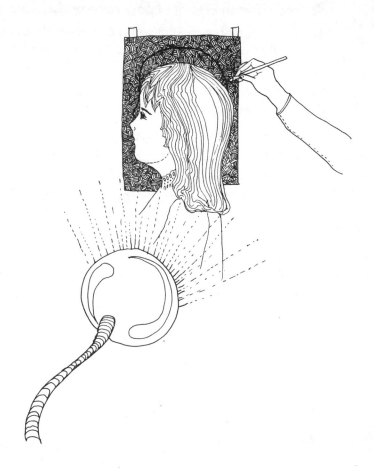

1 piece of black construction paper for each family member

1 lamp (a studio or desk lamp is fine)

White or tan parchmentlike paper (often called calligraphy papers in art stores)

One 9 × 12-inch glassed frame for each picture

Tape

Scissors

Pencil

Glue or dry mount tissue

1. Tape a piece of black paper to a wall. It should be at head height for each person.

2. Tip lamp so concentration of light is focused on black paper. Light should be at least 3 feet back from paper.

3. Place person in front of paper in a profile stance.

4. Adjust person and light so his or her profile is projected clearly onto black paper. You must get whole head onto the paper.

5. Trace the profile outline in pencil.

6. Cut out the silhouette.

7. Use glue or dry mount tissue to adhere the black silhouette to the white or tan parchmentlike paper.

8. Set mounted silhouette into frame.

9. Mount and frame a silhouette for each family member.

Soft Sculpture Anniversary Number (with caricatures)

You Need

2 soft sculpture faces. Add details to make them look like the couple (see directions on page 18).

1 yard of solid, calico, or gingham fabric (makes 3-4 numbers).

Needle or sewing machine

Color-coordinated thread

Pins

One-half 12-ounce bag polyester stuffing

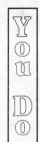

1. Use the number patterns on these pages. Enlarge to fit one digit on fabric. Trace pattern and cut two pieces for the same number.

2. Pin the two pieces together. Sew on wrong side of fabric ¼ in from edges. Clip curves and turn right-side out.

3. Stuff lightly with polyester stuffing and then slipstitch edges closed.

4. If you are making a two-digit number, say "22," tack the two numbers together with needle and thread.

5. Try various placements for the two heads. They look well together on a one-digit number and one high and one low on a two-digit number. (See illustration on page 157 for suggestions.) Use a needle and thread to tack on heads.

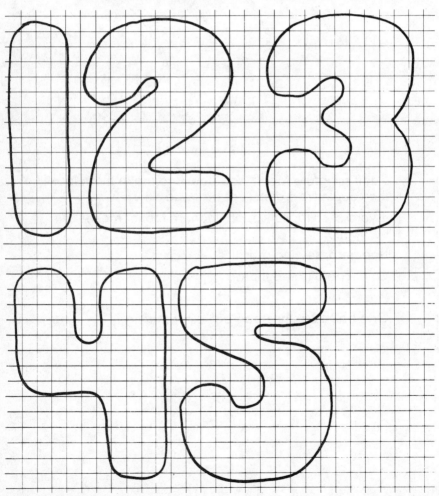

1 Square = 1 inch

Chapter 11

Gifts for the Home

Housewarmings

There is an adorable children's book about a little girl and her family who are about to move into a new neighborhood. Before they leave, they are given a going-away gift. In the new home, the little girl opens the gift and finds that it is a can opener. While her parents are busy moving boxes and furniture, the little girl goes into the kitchen and tries the new gift. She opens every can in the kitchen! Her parents walk in to find her surrounded with soup, chili, vegetables, macaroni, beans, and fruit. After their initial shock they decide to put the food to good use. They go around to all their new neighbors and invite them to supper! The little girl and that gift turned what was a rather lonely situation into a happy occasion, and an ordinary gift into a special one.

You can help friends who have ventured into new surroundings (and perhaps a new job or school) feel more at home with a gift that says welcome and congratulations.

ᒐᕒᕐ Put-together Suggestions ᕐᕔᕒ

- Brass or carved wood house numbers, together with molded chocolate or cookie numbers for them to eat. Include the molds or cutters as part of the gift.

- Hire a local artist to paint a design of their choice on the mailbox, or you paint the house numbers and a design on a large rock to use in their driveway. (Use acrylic paint and cover with at least three coats of polyurethane.)
- Ceramic tiles on which you've written (in permanent opaque markers) recipes that you've shared and enjoyed together. The tiles can be used as hot plates for the table or on a wall for decoration.
- A blackout emergency kit in a tote bag with any of the following: flashlight, long-lasting batteries, candles, inexpensive portable radio, matches, and bottled water.
- A coffee table book coordinated with their home style (country style, antique, or folk art book, for example).
- A bird feeder and bag of seeds or birdhouse.
- A hammock (and two sapling trees as a joke).
- Flower bulbs and a hand shovel to plant them.
- Seven of anything (the number 7 is universally thought of as a "lucky" number); for example, candles, candies, cookies, soaps, etc.
- A baby fruit tree you've planted and fertilized.
- A fireplace brush with a note attached, "Good for one chimney sweep. Call the company _____ to arrange for a convenient appointment."
- A log carrier with a few logs and long matches.
- For the new pool: something plastic (glasses, pitcher, trays), floating chairs, rafts, water games, motorized water toys, fancy beach towel, humorous pool signs, kerosene torches, night lights, or an insect repellent kit (citronella candles, punks, sprays, lotions, yellow light bulbs, smoke coils, all packed in a safari hat wrapped with mosquito netting).
- Food in a fancy container for them to keep; for example, ice cream with scoop, dishes and all the trimmings; or liqueur and glasses; pie on a pie plate, etc.
- A helping hand (yours) with a purchased gift that symbolizes your gift of time and energy; for example, a bucket of paint and an offer to help paint a room; videotape and offer to tape an inventory of their valuables; or a progress report on remodeling.
- A subscription to their hometown newspaper.

Gifts of Welcome to a New Neighborhood

The best gift to give to someone new in the neighborhood is still a smile with a warm handshake. Yet housewarming gifts can also be the means of introducing ourselves and saying, "Welcome."

- A subscription to the new town's newspaper "from all of your neighbors on Kings Highway" with a list of new neighbor's names and phone numbers.
- Road maps or a road map book of the area with important places indicated with red marks.

Welcome Basket

This is a lovely way to introduce everyone in the neighborhood to the new neighbors.

You Need

1 medium- to large-sized basket with handle

1 contribution of some of following from each neighbor (crackers, cheeses, jams, teas/coffees, candies, baked goods, wines, etc.)

Clear plastic wrap

3–4 yards of ¼-inch ribbon

1½ yards of 1-inch ribbon

3 × 5-inch index cards

Hole puncher

1. Call each of the neighbors and let them choose one gift for the new neighbors.

2. Collect all items and loosely wrap in gathered clear plastic wrap. Tie a knot on each item with ¼-inch ribbon and fill out a tag, then slip on ribbon and finish with a bow.

3. Each tag is a folded 3 × 5 card that says, "From your neighbors, the _____ at # _____.

4. Use the large ribbon to tie a bow on the basket handle and a tag that says, "Welcome to _____ Street."

5. Include a list of names and phone numbers of all contributing neighbors.

Variation: Organize a progressive street dinner. Each neighbor prepares part of a dinner as you all go from house to house sharing good food and chatter.

Personalized Yellow Pages

Imagine having just moved into a new town and not being sure where you can get your prescriptions filled, buy pastries, or find a dentist. The first place you would look is the Yellow Pages, of course.

Personalized Yellow Pages and a local map make this search even easier.

A scrapbook or blank page book (buy)

3 × 5 cards

Typewriter

Markers

1. Pass out a set of 3 × 5 cards to several area friends or neighbors on which to list their favorite:

- Drugstore
- Clothing store
- Shoe store
- Grocery store
- Gift store
- Department store
- Doctor (internist and pediatrician)
- Dentist
- Restaurant
- Take-out restaurant
- Entertainment

Annotations could include: best prices, always double coupons, practices general medicine, gourmet items, etc.

2. Group the cards into categories in the scrapbook—drugstores, clothing, doctors, entertainment, food stores, restaurants.

3. Staple in cards. You can also type information on sheets and glue in rather than use the cards.

4. Make a map (or use a commerical one of your locality obtained from the real estate agency or your local Chamber of Commerce). Mark the places mentioned.

5. You might want to include a gift certificate to one store on the list.

Personalized Napkins

1 yard cotton polyester or all-synthetic fabric, or purchase plain napkins

Your choice of appliqué, stencil, embroidery, iron-on transfer paint for decoration

Small basket

Needle and thread

Glue (hot glue gun or white tacky)

1. Measure and cut six napkins sized 15 × 15 inches.

2. For a formal napkin, hem as follows:
   Fold raw edge ¼ inch and machine stitch all around. Again fold edges in ½ inch, tucking sewn edge under. Hand hem or machine stitch all around.

3. For a casual, informal type-napkin, hem as follows:
   Sew a long, machine stay stitch around napkin about ⅝ inch in from edges. This will prevent too much fraying. Use an ordinary pin to pry out threads along all edges. Pull the threads out and discard. Continue pulling threads until fringe measures ½ inch.

4. Personalize each napkin with the name or initials of each family member in an outline embroidery stitch. Use your choice of decorative technique to add a special design for each person. (See page 175 for some design suggestions.)

5. Place in a small basket which you've lined with a scrap of the same fabric or another coordinated piece of fabric.

How to Line the Basket

1. Measure with a tape measure the depth of the basket from the outside top edge to the bottom flat surface. Add that measurement to one-half the measurement across the basket's bottom. Now add one more inch. This will be the width of your fabric piece.

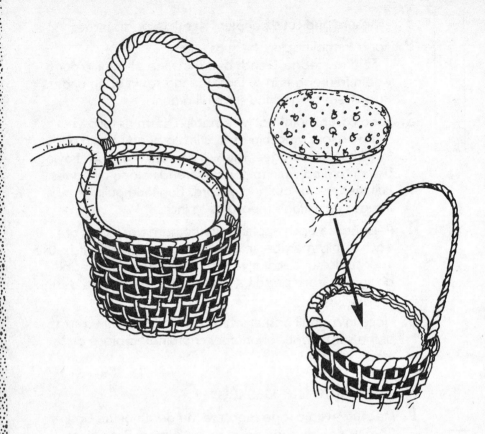

2. To get the measurement of length, pull the tape measure along inside basket rim. Add 1 inch.

3. Cut fabric to your individual basket's measurements.

4. Fold down one long edge ½" and machine stitch. Do the same for the opposite long edge.

5. Along one of these hemmed edges, sew a basting stitch and pull strings to gather it. Turn fabric right side inward.

6. Seam up short edges, sewing ½ inch from raw edges.

7. Place liner in basket so that right side of fabric shows and all raw edges are concealed. Gathered part is at the bottom of the basket.

8. Glue (using hot glue gun or white tacky glue) top edge of fabric to inside rim of basket.

Optional: Include a small book on the art of napkin folding.

Bread Dough Breadbasket

This is a beautiful yet useful gift. It can actually hold rolls, crackers, or bread. It is time-consuming to make, but the pleasure expressed by the receiver will make it well worth your time.

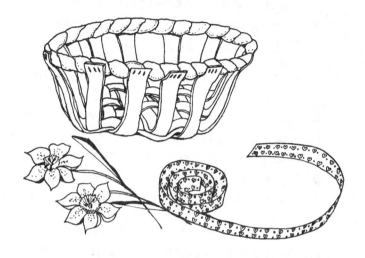

4 cups flour

1¾ cups warm water

1 cup iodized salt

Shortening

Clear plastic wrap

2 quart round oven-proof bowl

Baking sheet

Shortening

Ruler

Knife or pizza cutter

Fork

Toothpick

Polyurethane (Zip-Guard)

Brush

1. Combine salt, flour, and slowly add warm water.

2. Mix well and knead 8 minutes. Keep dough covered at all times with plastic wrap when you are not actually handling it.

3. Invert a round oven-proof bowl on a greased baking sheet. Grease the bowl and sheet well.

4. Take two pieces of dough tennis-ball size and roll into long (36 inches long and ¾ inch thick) "snakes." Twist them together (see step A), and place around inverted lip of bowl. With water, wet both ends where they meet.

5. Roll out remaining dough to ¼-inch thickness.

6. Use a ruler and mark strips ¾ inch wide. Cut long strips with a knife or pizza cutter. (See step B.)

7. Place strips over bowl, weaving them as in a basket. Place one layer of strips over bowl first, then weave a layer on top. (See step C.) Attach ends (with water) to twisted edges and trim away excess.

8. Press fork tines into the edges of each strip for strength and decoration. (See step D.)

9. Use a toothpick and prick each crossed strip for better cooking.

10. Place in 300° oven. Bake 1½–2 hours. Then remove basket and bowl from oven and turn basket over on baking sheet. Carefully take bowl out.

11. Continue cooking basket alone in an upright position for another hour or until very hard.

12. Let cool for a day, then brush with three or four coats of polyurethane.

Bread Dough Breadbasket

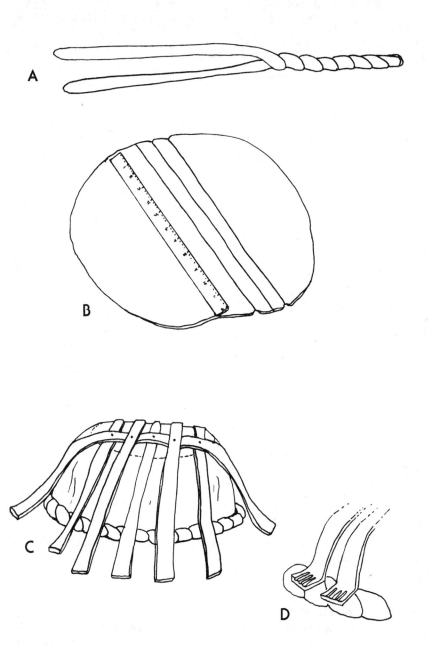

A

B

C

D

Personalized Mugs

Nothing appeals more to people than seeing their names and symbols of things they love on an item they can use every day.

You Need

1 light-colored ceramic or stoneware mug for each family member

Fine-line Deco Color pens in your choice of colors

You Do

1. Write name on mug.
2. Draw symbol(s) of something the person loves, of an interest, or hobby.
3. These mugs are hand washable. Do not put them in the dishwasher.
4. Optional: fill with flowers or candy.

Variations:
- For a student at school: if there's a roommate make another one with his/her name on it. Make an extra that says, "For a Friend!"
- For Christmas: Let each family member decorate his/her own at your holiday dinner. The mugs can be reused each year.

Herbal Wreath

This naturally beautiful gift is actually a useful kitchen addition as well. Herbs can be detached and used for cooking.

You Need

1 small-sized grapevine wreath

1 package thin floral wire

2 yards ¼-inch ribbon in your choice of color

Needle and thread

Sprigs of dried herbs: parsley, basil, thyme, mint, dill, rosemary, oregano

15 bay leaves

½ × ¾-inch cardboard tags

Folded 5 × 7 card

1. Gather small sprigs of herbs. Tie a bow made with 9 inches of ribbon around bottom stems. Make eight small sprigs of various herbs.

2. Write the name of each herb on a tiny label. Use needle and thread to attach to sprig.

3. Attach herbs to wreath with floral wire twisted around grapevines. Place equally around wreath.

4. Place five bay leaves together to form a flower shape. Use needle and thread to sew them together at their center point.

5. Poke two ends of one piece of floral wire through center and twist around grapevines.

6. Make two more bay leaf "flowers" and attach around wreath.

7. Write one of the following messages on the 5 × 7 card, or add a recipe that you like:

The Language of Herbs

Rosemary means remembrance
Parsley means festivity
Sage means esteem
Thyme means sweetness
Mint means virtue and wisdom

Creative Ways to Cook with Herbs

Parsley—Season vegetables, soups, salads with meats, fish and eggs.
Basil—Flavor tomato dishes, meats such as beef, lamb, and poultry.
Thyme—Sprinkle in soups, stews, chowders, and meat dishes.
Mint—Brew mint teas.
Dill—Use to flavor pickles and dilled (or cooked) vegetables such as coleslaw. Use with mayonnaise for fish dips. Flowers, leaves, or seeds used to make dill vinegar.
Rosemary—Strong flavor for meats and soups.
Oregano—Add to tomato dishes.

Framed Photo

This photo can be created in a variety of ways, yet the final result is the same. It is a lasting memory of a time in our lives that we shared with good friends.

35mm camera and film
Photo processing
Frame to fit enlarged photo
Craft knife
Dry mount tissue

Choice 1. Take a photo of the moving family's home with all the neighbors gathered around the front of it. A good time to get everyone together is usually late Sunday morning. Enlarge to desired size and frame. Enlargement can be expensive, but it's well worth it. Check the prices at large photo labs.

Choice 2. Collage—Take a photo of the moving family's home. Take individual closeup, full body photos of families and friends. Make copies of people photos in regular size. Make one enlargement of house. With a craft knife, cut around outline of each family. Use dry mount tissue between house photo and family photo and iron into place around home.

Choice 3. Montage—Have some fun with this. Again take individual photos of home and close-up photos of friends. Enlarge home photo. Use craft knife to cut away background on people and dry mount them to windows, door, chimney, or cut open the windows, door and chimney and mount photos behind each.

Bread Dough Wreath

This wall decoration makes a lovely kitchen adornment. It has the natural look of bread dough yet is sturdy enough to last for years.

You Need

4 cups flour

1 cup iodized salt

1¾ cup warm water

Cloves

Shortening

Clear plastic wrap

2 pieces heavy (18- or 20-gauge) floral wire

Baking sheet

Rolling pin

Pie crimper (with fluted edges)

Toothpick

Polyurethane (Zip-Guard)

Brush

1. Mix flour and salt well.

2. Slowly add water and mix into a stiff dough. (Test the correct consistency of the dough by holding in one hand. If it oozes downward very slowly, it is just right. If it doesn't move at all, it is too dry, so add 2 tablespoons more water. If it falls quickly, add 2 to 4 tablespoons more flour.)

3. Knead dough until very smooth (8 minutes). Keep dough covered with plastic wrap at all times when not working with it.

4. Twist wires together at ends to make one large circle. In the middle of one wire twist one loop. This will be used for hanging the finished wreath. This loop is at the top of the wreath.

5. Place the wire on a greased baking sheet.

6. Roll 18–24-inch-long and 2-inch-wide "snake." It should be ½ inch thick. Pat it over the circular wire. Conceal all the wire except the hanging loop. Adhere the two ends together with water.

7. Roll out a good-sized piece of dough to ¼ inch thickness. Use pie crimper to cut leaves about 1½ × 2 inches. Press "veins" into leaves with a toothpick. Place leaves in groups of two's or three's around dough wreath. *Important:* Always attach one piece of dough to another with water.

8. Roll balls of dough in hand to form grapes, oranges, apples, pears, apricots, and bananas.

9. Add details to fruits as follows:

   toothpick pricks all over the orange

   clove stem on apple with four toothpick creases around top

   a piece of clove stem for pear and cluster grapes

   a toothpick crease on apricot

10. Attach all pieces with water.

11. Bake in 300° oven for 1½ to 2 hours until it is hard to the touch.

12. Let dry for a day and cover with three coats of brushed-on polyurethane.

Invited to Dinner?

We were taught that we *had* to write "bread-and-butter" notes to say thank you and *had* to bring "bread-and-butter" gifts to someone's home to thank them for dinner invitations or overnight stays. The notes were mandatory and the proper dinner gifts had to be flowers, candy, or wine.

Today, there are fewer "have-to-do's" and more "want-to-do's." We want to bring gifts to dinner to express our gratitude for the invitation, knowing that the host or hostess has taken the time and trouble to plan an entertaining time for us.

⌇⌇ Put-together Suggestions ⌇⌇

Gifts of Food

Gifts of food should be given with the idea that the family can enjoy them at another time. Most hosts and hostesses have their menu all set and would prefer not to make last-minute changes to accommodate your gift unless it was requested (you offered in advance) and they are expecting it.

A gift of food is always appreciated:

- An especially desired item (bag of favorite nuts).
- A luxury item (caviar, fresh fruit dipped in chocolate—see directions on page 184).
- Your homemade specialty (bread, cake).
- An addition to the ordinary (butter crock with herbs to make herb butter; cinnamon sticks with spiced tea, mulled cider and hot chocolate drink recipes; a mustard crock with imported gourmet mustard; a bottle of wine and a wine coaster, unusual corkscrew, clay cooler, or wine book; popcorn in an antique tin).

Gifts for the Home

Bring any small item to be used in the home—just make it beautiful, different, or fun, and related in some way to the family's interests or likes.

- Unusual kitchen utensil (egg separator, orange peeler, strawberry huller, grate scraper, pie crimper, spaghetti measurer, set of chopsticks and/or chopstick rests, kitchen or gardening sheers, fancy ice cube trays).
- Flower bulbs in a bag or container of gravel and soil to force open.
- An unusual plant like the Venus's flytrap that can be fed.
- An herb plant with tiny scissors and recipe attached to it.
- Milk/water pitcher filled with flowers.

Fun Gifts You Can Add On Each Time You Visit

- Start an animal collection; for example, cows or pigs in potholders, magnets, napkin rings, wall decorations, etc.
- An unusual shaped/designed salt and pepper shaker; bring a different kind each time.
- Logs for their fireplace tied with a ribbon.

Gifts for the Family

Bring a gift the whole family can enjoy or small individual gifts for the children such as:

- Refrigerator magnets personalized by gluing a photo of each family member onto the front. (The heart-shaped ones work well.)
- A photo framed or collaged of the last time you were together.
- Small individual gifts to their children; something usable like marking pens and note pads, cans of play dough, bubble jars, stickers, or a game for the whole family.

Pretzels and Fruits Dipped in Chocolate

In few minutes, you can create an elegant gift that anyone would be delighted to receive.

12 ounces of real semisweet chocolate chips

2 tablespoons shortening

Small package of small-sized, thin pretzels (traditional style)

A few assorted fruits (fresh whole strawberries, dried apricot halves, or other dried fruits)

2 saucepans (one larger than the other) or double boiler

Fork

Skewer

Waxed paper

1. Melt chocolate in top part of double boiler. Add shortening.

2. Dip each pretzel into melted chocolate, covering completely. Place on skewer and rest skewer across the edge of the chocolate saucepan. (Any drips will go right back into the chocolate.) Dip all the pretzels you like.

3. Dip strawberries and dried fruits in chocolate, leaving a small section undipped.

Herb Vinegars

The beautiful smells and sight of fresh herbs can be preserved in wonderful gifts of herb vinegars. More than just attractive, they are delicious on salads. They will last for a whole winter season, yet are best when used within the first two months of being made.

Fresh herbs (check for combinations)

White, red and/or cider vinegar

Clear bottles with cork stoppers (corks are available in hardware stores)

Labels (see label designs on p. 187)

White glue (Elmer's)

1. Prepare bottles by washing well with soapy water. Rinse well with cold water. Boil 5 minutes (for sturdy bottles) or pour boiling water in bottles and let set 5 minutes.

2. Pick herbs in the morning before the hot sun is on them.

3. Immediately rinse each herb and place a sprig in bottle.

4. Fill bottle to top with appropriate vinegar.

5. Cork top and let brew in sunlight for 2 days or let stand for 2 weeks in a dark place.

6. Reproduce the labels on facing page and glue onto bottles with white (Elmer's) glue.

erb and Vinegar Chart

HERB	VINEGAR
Tarragon sprig	Red or cider
Dill stem and flower	White
Oregano sprig	Red or white
Parsley stalks	Red or white
Basil leaves	Red
Basil leaves, clove garlic, and sprig of thyme	White
Rosemary sprig	White
Mint leaves	White
Thyme	White
Chive blossoms	White

Herb Garden in a Basket

Prepare this bountiful basket for a friend. The herbs can be transferred outside in the warm weather.

1 shallow basket with handle

Heavy-duty aluminum foil

A few potted herbs such as dwarf basil, winter thyme, rosemary, and oregano

1 yard of gingham checked ribbon

1. Line the basket with two sheets of heavy-duty aluminum foil.

2. Place the herbs and pots in the basket.

3. Tie a big bow on the handle.

Variation: Herb Plant with Scissors and Recipe
Tie a bow around a pot of herbs. Use 18 inches of ¼-inch ribbon so one side is left very long. Attach a small pair of scissors to the long end. Place a recipe card in the plant.

Sprout or Herb Message

With a few days advance notice you can "sprout" a personal message to friends. They will enjoy both seeing your unique means of communication as well as using the sprouts in salads.

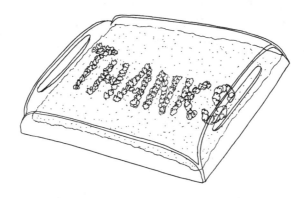

A shallow container (such as a planter, cake or bread loaf pan, tray)

Clear plastic wrap

Small bag of potting soil

Alfalfa or mung seeds

Plant mister

12-inch yarn or ribbon piece

1. Line container with plastic wrap. This will keep it clean so container can be reused, especially in the case of a pan or tray.

2. Place soil in container to the depth of 1 to 2 inches.

3. Decide on a message or picture design you'd like to convey. For example, you might want to say "Thanks" or design a picture appropriate to the season.

4. Very lightly press your design or saying into the loose soil.

5. Sprinkle the alfalfa seeds or place the mung seeds into the slight impressions.

6. Cover with ¹⁄₁₆ inch of finely sprinkled soil.

7. Moisten well with a plant mister.

8. Cover with plastic wrap and set aside for 3 to 4 days or until it sprouts.

9. Wrap entire container in plastic wrap, gather at the top, and tie with a ribbon or yarn bow.

Variation: Use herb seeds such as basil, dill, or parsley in place of alfalfa or mung sprouts. It will take longer for these to sprout through the soil, however. Once growing, they can be continually clipped and used for cooking. Follow seed packet directions for planting.

Hand-Dipped Pressed-Flower Candles

Hand-dipped pressed-flower candles are a beautiful gift to hang as decorations or to light up a dining table.

You Need

2 packages of paraffin (available in grocery stores) or paraffin plus beeswax. (This comes in slabs and is found only in some craft stores. It is expensive, but makes a finer candle.)

Wicking (1 package of medium sized, found only in craft stores)

Old pieces of wax crayons in colors you will be making the candles. (Use approximately 2 whole crayons for each container of wax.)

Two 1-pound tin coffee cans

2-pound tin coffee can

Dried pressed flowers (leaves optional)

Pins (optional)

Old wooden spoon

Toilet tissue

1. Place chunks of paraffin in a 1-pound coffee can. Place this can into the 2-pound coffee can which is partially filled with water.

2. Place over heat source until water starts to boil. Lower and watch carefully as wax melts. *Never* melt wax directly over heat—the wax can must be placed in boiling water. Wax is ready when it is melted clear. Do not let it become too hot, because it will be difficult to work with. Also, you can add the crayon pieces now for color. Stir with a wooden spoon.

3. Fill the other 1-pound can to the top with cold water.

4. Remove wax and water cans from heat source and place next to the cold water can.

5. Cut a piece of wicking 18 inches long. Hold the center of it in your hand so both ends are draping down but not close together.

6. Dip both ends into hot wax. The first dip will be slow as you wait for the wicks to sink. All succeeding dips should be done very quickly in and out of the hot wax. Let the hot wax drips go back into the hot wax. (See step A.) Then plunge the wax-covered wicks quickly into the cold water to set. Leave for about 10 seconds and pull out. Gently wipe candle with a piece of toilet tissue to remove water droplets. Straighten the wicks and dip in can of wax as far down as wick will go without bending.

7. Continue dipping in hot wax, then cold water until you've built up two good-sized candles. (See step B.) Let candles cool by hanging them for about 30 minutes.

8. After you've dipped candles, place dried flowers or leaves around candle and use pins, stuck into candle, to hold down each part. (See step C.) Dip candles into hot wax once more. Let set in air for 10 seconds and remove pins. Dip into hot wax once more and let cool thoroughly. This variation makes a beautiful, subtle change in hand-dipped candles.

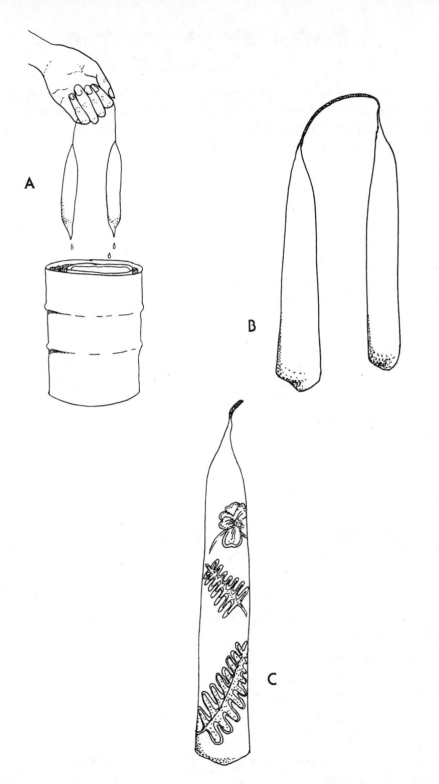

A

B

C

Sunshine Sugar People Cookies

If you enjoy cookie baking, whip up a batch of these lemony cutouts. Make each cookie look like a family member with the addition of a painted frosting. Pack your cookie family in a basket and tote them out to dinner!

⅓ cup vegetable oil

¾ cup sugar

1 tablespoon grated lemon peel

1 tablespoon lemon juice

1 egg

1½ cup unbleached flour

1 teaspoon baking powder

Pinch salt

Plastic wrap

Egg paint made with 1 egg yolk and ¼ cup confectioners' sugar

Food colors

Sharp knife or people cookie cutters

1 new (or super clean) craft paint brush, size 0 or 1

Paper or cloth napkin

1 rectanglular-shaped basket with handle (approximately 8 inches × 5 inches)

18 inches of ribbon (to tie a bow on handle)

1. In a medium bowl, combine oil, sugar, lemon peel, and juice, and beat well.

2. Add 1 egg and beat.

3. Add baking powder and salt to flour and add all to above lemon juice mixture.

4. Ball up dough and wrap in plastic wrap. Refrigerate for at least 1 hour.

5. Roll dough out to ⅛-inch thick on a lightly floured surface. Use cookie cutters or cut a "people" shape about 6 inches tall with a sharp knife. If you use the knife, you can individualize each cookie by height, body shape (please, be complimentary only!), hairstyle, and choice of clothing.

6. Place on ungreased cookie sheets and bake at 375° for 8 to 10 minutes.

7. Cool thoroughly on wire racks.

8. Meanwhile, beat up 1 egg yolk with ¼ cup confectioners' sugar. Divide the mixture between four or five small dishes. Tint each dish with a few drops of food color to make colors of your choice—brown (red and green), yellow, red, blue, green.

9. Paint features on cookies with brush to resemble real family to whom you are bringing the cookies. Remember to add glasses, familiar style of clothing, hair colors, and so on. Let frosting dry until hard.

10. Place cookies in a paper napkin-lined basket and tie a ribbon bow on the handle.

Chapter 12

Get-Well Gifts

Taking the time to visit an ill friend or relative is an act of caring, and our presence is the most precious gift we can give. Still, a gift serves many purposes: it can help fill up the hours of convalescence; it can make the person laugh and lift his spirits; and it can be a cheerful part of us that stays, even after visiting is over.

✦✦✦ Put-together Suggestions ✦✦✦

Gifts to Help Pass Time

- Crossword puzzles with a dictionary, atlas, almanac, pencils and erasers.
- A deck of cards and a book on solitaire.
- Nail polish assortment and nail grooming kit.
- Sketch pad, markers, and colored pencils, and real flowers to sketch.
- Radio or cassette player and earphone and tapes with messages from family and friends.
- TV rental for a week with a *TV Guide*.
- Stationery, pens, address book, and stamps, plus a bed tray or lap desk.

Gifts that Make Connections to Home and Friends

- Collaged pictures in a frame (which you can change with each visit).
- Get-well banner—have everyone sign it.
- Heartfelt message board. (Have relatives and friends send in messages on felt hearts that you have distributed. Display them on bulletin board in patient's room.)

Gifts for Raising Spirits

- Art or travel posters.
- Theater tickets, date for lunch (your treat), and shopping (for when the patient gets well).
- Something silly—a stuffed animal (for company) plus a helium balloon with the get-well message attached to the bottom.
- Something new and fun to wear always feels good—a personalized night T-shirt that has best wishes written all over it in indelible ink, a humorous shower cap, or animal slippers.
- A bath rest pillow and waterproof book, for example, a shower songbook.
- Gifts of service and time to help free a patient's mind of some of those special worries and concerns that often accompany an illness: entertain their children for a day; care for plants or pets; tidy up their home; run errands (request a list).

Pocket Pillow

Here is a practical yet decorative gift to make and give someone confined to bed. Just looking at the cheery designs makes one feel good.

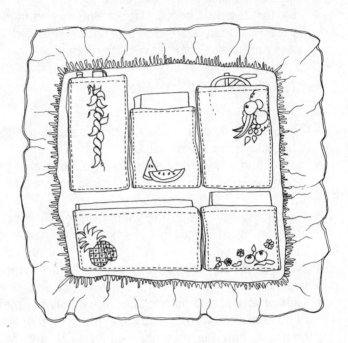

¾ yard of solid-colored cotton or cotton/polyester fabric
Acrylic or fabric paint
Fine-bristled brushes
Fine-pointed permanent pen (Sharpie)
One 12-ounce bag polyester stuffing

1. Measure and cut out two pieces of fabric. Each should be 14 inches square. (This will be the pillow.)

2. Cut two strips of fabric. Each should be 6½ inches wide × 45 inches long. Cut another strip 6½ inches wide × 12 inches long. (These are for the ruffle.)

3. Cut remaining piece of fabric into the following sizes for pockets: (See diagram.)

   a 5 × 4 inches (pad)
   b 7 inches × 4 inches (tissues)
   c 6 inches × 5 inches (glasses holder)
   d 3 inches × 7 inches (pencils/pens)
   e 5 inches × 5 inches (deck of cards)

4. Use acrylic or fabric paints and fine-bristled brush to apply designs to pocket pieces. (See diagram on following page for designs and placements.) Let dry.

5. Use fine-pointed permanent pen to add a few outlines and details.

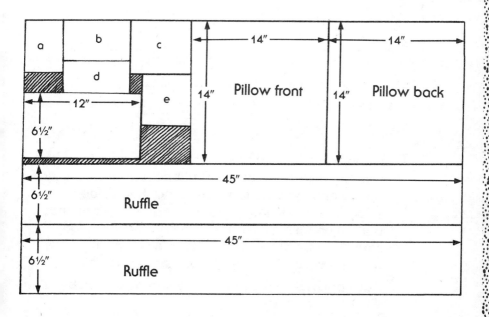

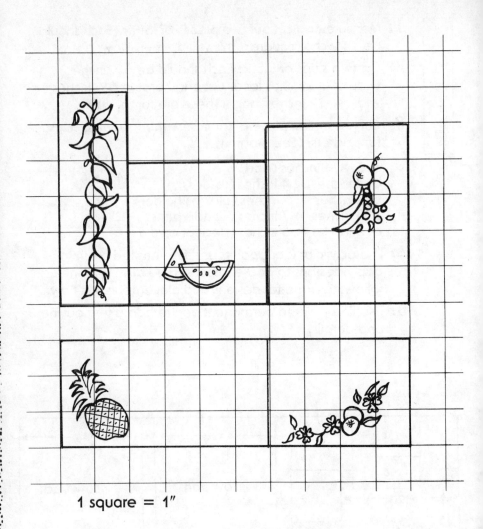

1 square = 1″

6. Prepare patch pocket pieces for sewing on pillow. Start with the 6 × 5-inch piece. Fold back and down ½ inch on top and machine topstitch ¼ inch from folded edge. Fold back and upward ½ inch of fabric on the bottom and pin. Fold back ½ inch of fabric on each long side and pin. Repeat with all other patch pocket pieces, taking ½-inch hems. Iron each smooth.

7. Place pockets on one 14-inch square piece of fabric as shown. Pin in place.

8. With a long machine stitch, sew along the two sides and bottom of each patch pocket about ¼ inch from edge.

9. To make ruffle:

(a.) Sew the three 6½-inch strips of fabric together end to end to make one long strip.
(b.) Fold strip in half so ruffle is 3¼ inches wide. Iron.
(c.) Sew a basting stitch along raw edges about ¼ inch.
(d.) Pull threads to make gentle gathers.

10. Pin ruffle around edge of 14-inch square with pockets. Ruffle should face inward.

11. Place second 14-inch square on top. Stitch all around ½ inch in from edge. Leave 4 inches open to turn.

12. Turn pillow. Stuff. Slip stitch closed.

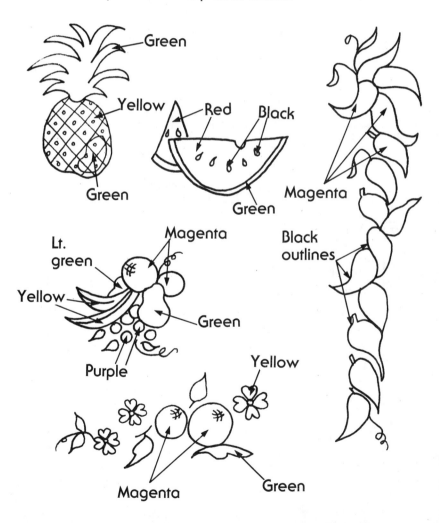

Mason Jar Gardens

These jars of quick-sprouting seeds can be enjoyed each day. They grow roots and stems rapidly and provide something to look at. The patient will look forward to checking out their progress each morning.

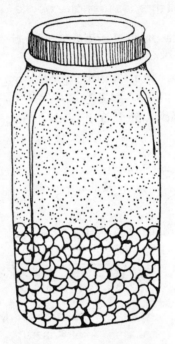

1 quart-sized, widemouth mason (canning) jar with top

½ cup gravel

½ cup sand

3 cups potting soil

Quick-growing seeds such as green pole beans, radish, popcorn kernels

Small watering can

1. Place sand in bottom of jar.
2. Gently add gravel on top of sand.
3. Fill rest of jar with soil right up to top of rim.
4. Place seeds around glass rim in soil. This will allow patient to watch the fascinating root growth system as well as the above-soil growth. Sprinkle with a little soil to cover each seed.
5. Cover tightly and give to patient, together with a small watering can and instructions for patient to water jar, replace cap loosely for two days and place it in the sun. After two days remove cap and water when dry.

Patient opens lid and waters the seeds in the jar. Soon roots and tips will sprout and provide a lovely green garden at the top of the jar. Because of its tiny size, the plants will be mostly decorative, although there could be a small radish and maybe a bean or two.

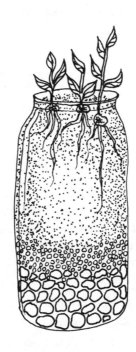

Chocolate Message

Words have never been so sweet! Write your own get well message in delicate chocolate letters.

6 ounces semisweet chocolate bits
1 tablespoon melted vegetable shortening
or
½ pound chocolate melting caps
Heat proof glass jar
Saucepan
Squeeze bottle (such as a super-clean mustard container)
Waxed paper

1. Melt the chocolate bits and vegetable shortening or the melting caps in the jar over simmering water in a saucepan. Spoon melted chocolate into squeeze bottle. (If you have a microwave oven, put the bits and shortening or the melting caps directly into the squeeze bottle and microwave at HI for 1½ to 2 minutes.)

2. Let cool for 2–3 minutes with cap off.

3. With a steady pressure, squeeze the chocolate onto waxed paper in your choice of message. If chocolate becomes too hard, set squeeze bottle into bowl of hot water.

4. Set in freezer for 5 minutes. Peel from waxed paper.

Basket of Hearts

These hearts have get-well wishes written all over them. You may want to stuff one with potpourri for a fragrant reminder of your love and concern.

(TO MAKE 4 HEARTS)

¼ yard each of muslin and printed calico

2 yards of ½-inch lace trim

Needle and thread

6 ounces polyester stuffing

Potpourri (optional)

Pencil

Fine-tipped permanent marking pens

Basket, approximately 10 × 8 inches wide × 4 inches deep with handle (available in florist, basket, or gift shops)

18 inches of 1-inch wide ribbon for basket trim

1. Trace or copy the heart pattern in step A on facing page onto folded paper. Cut it out.

2. Place heart pattern on muslin. Trace with a pencil. Cut out fabric heart.

3. Place heart pattern on calico. Trace with a pencil. Cut out fabric heart.

4. Cut an 18-inch piece of lace. Pin lace so that it is facing inward around the edge of the right side of the calico heart, as shown in step B.

5. Sew a running stitch through calico and lace about ⅛ inch from the edge.

6. Place muslin heart on top of lace, and pin. Sew together ¼ inch in from edge of heart. Leave a 1½-inch opening near bottom.

7. Clip edges all around heart as shown in step C.

8. Turn heart right side out. Stuff with polyester.

9. Add some potpourri with the polyester, if desired.

10. Slip stitch the open edge closed (step D).

11. Write your message on the muslin side with a permanent marker.

12. Put hearts in basket, trim basket with a bow, using the 18-inch piece of ribbon.

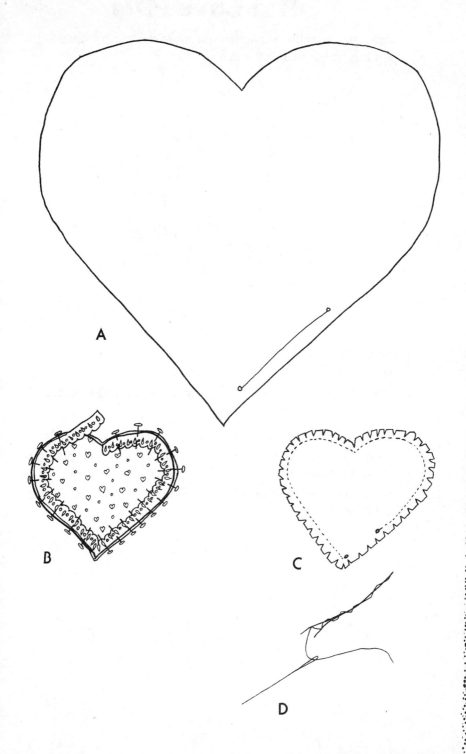

A

B

C

D

Rx: Love Pills

This humorous but loving gift will make the patient smile . . .
perhaps with a tear in the eye.

Pills, in aspirin or aspirin substitute size

Photos of family and friends (tiny faces, as in group shots)

Ball-point pen

White tacky glue

A pillbox, regular type or the weekly kind with a compartment for each day

A small piece of lightweight cardboard, or colored construction paper for card

Tape

1. Place the pill over a photo of the face of someone you want to include in your pillbox.

2. Trace around the face with a ball-point pen. Cut out picture on inside of pen line.

3. Attach the photo to the pill with tacky glue. Let dry.

4. Continue attaching photos to pills until you have as many as you want included, or one for each day if you are using a weekly box.

5. Place pills in pillbox, photo side up.

6. Cut cardboard or construction paper to fit in lid of pillbox or on the bottom.

7. Write this prescription on the piece of cardboard: "Get well soon, our love is your BEST medicine."

8. Tape card to bottom or inside of pillbox.

Good Luck Charms

Through the ages, humans have endowed various objects and symbols with supposed magical qualities which they believe will bring them good luck or protect them from evil.

Make up a box of good luck charms. Even the staunchest realist will appreciate your signs of affection and gifts of hope.

Oven-baked clay (Fimo or Sculpey III), 1 package each of red, blue, and yellow

Toothpick for modeling clay

One 6-inch square of white felt fabric

Pink embroidery thread and embroidery needle

Needle and thread

Polyester stuffing

1 yard of ¼-inch red ribbon

One 6-inch square piece of calico

A coin—a special one such as a silver dollar or a British sixpence

A clean, well-scrubbed wishbone; tied with a ribbon bow

Pin backings or magnet pieces

Hot glue gun

Attractive box, approximately 4 × 6 inches, in material of your choice

How to Make a Rainbow

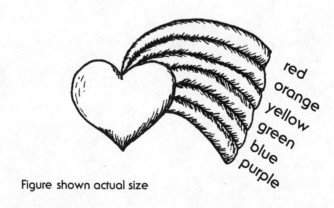

red
orange
yellow
green
blue
purple

Figure shown actual size

1. Use oven-baked clay to mold a heart about 1 inch wide.

2. Continue to use clay to mold a rainbow from red, red and yellow mixed to make orange, yellow, yellow and blue mixed to make green, blue, and red and blue mixed to make purple. Roll each color into a 2-inch snake. Stick together, in rainbow fashion, with a little pressure and arch slightly (as shown in illustration on facing page).

3. Press heart over edge of left side of rainbow, as shown.

4. Bake according to directions on clay package. Let cool.

5. Heat glue stick in gun. Place a thick dab of hot glue on back near top of charm. Quickly imbed the pin backing or magnet. Press to secure tightly. Let cool.

How to Make Four-Leaf Clover:

Figure shown actual size

1. Use oven-baked clay to mold four hearts, each about ½ inch wide, from green clay (mix the yellow and blue well, and knead).

2. Roll a green snake about 1 inch long. Flatten slightly to form the stem.

3. Press hearts, points together, to form a four-leaf clover (see illustration above). Press onto stem.

4. Bake according to directions on clay package. Let cool.

5. Heat glue stick in your gun. Place a thick dab of hot glue on back near top of clover. Quickly imbed the pin backing or magnet. Press to secure tightly. Let cool.

How to Make a Horseshoe

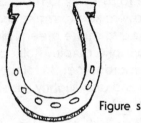

Figure shown actual size

1. Mix together and knead equal amounts of yellow and blue oven-baked clay to make green. Add an equal amount of red to make brown.

2. Roll into a 3-inch snake. Flatten and taper ends. Shape into a horseshoe.

3. Poke small holes in a row all along top surface to resemble nail holes, as shown in illustration above.

4. Bake according to directions on clay package. Let cool.

5. Heat glue stick in gun. Place a thick dab of hot glue on back of horseshoe. Quickly imbed magnet only. (Pin won't work because horseshoe has to be held with open end upward so that luck doesn't run out.) Press tightly to secure. Let cool.

How to Make a Rabbit's Foot (take the whole rabbit, please!)

Figure shown actual size

1. Trace the pattern on facing page onto a piece of tracing paper.

2. Trace pattern onto two pieces of white felt. Cut out two felt rabbits.

3. Use pink embroidery thread (two strands) to sew (in outline stitch) a nose, whiskers, eyes, tummy line, and paw lines onto one felt rabbit, as shown.

4. Place the two rabbit-shaped pieces of felt back to back and stitch all around edges with a running stitch. Add small amounts of polyester stuffing as you stitch so rabbit is slightly puffy.

5. Roll a ½-inch ball of polyester stuffing tightly and tack onto back with needle and thread for a tail.

6. Cut a 6-inch piece of red ribbon. Tie it into a small bow. Tack the bow onto the ankle of one foot with needle and thread.

How to Make Lucky Numbers

Figure shown actual size

1. Use the guide on page 158 to make a paper pattern of the patient's lucky number. (Do *not* enlarge.)

2. Fold a piece of calico double and trace around the pattern. Cut out the fabric number. Place pieces right sides together.

3. Stitch around ¼ inch from edge of number leaving about 2 inches open.

4. Clip curved edges and turn.

5. Stuff lightly with polyester.

6. Slip stitch closed.

Assemble all of the charms of your choice (rainbow, wishbone and/or four-leaf clover, horseshoe, rabbit's foot, lucky number(s), wishbone, and/or coin) into box. Enclose gift card that says, "Use these magical good luck charms to hold onto, to believe in (as we do), and for wishing you a speedy recovery."

Figure shown actual size

Resources

The following is a partial listing of mail order catalogs we have found to be useful sources for gifts and ideas.

Museums and Organizations

Brooklyn Museum Gallery Shop
Eastern Parkway
Brooklyn, NY 11238

The Cathedral Shop
Church of St. John the Divine
1047 Amsterdam Avenue
New York, NY 10025

Center for Environmental Education
624 9th Street NW
Washington, DC 20001

Discovery Corner
Lawrence Hall of Science
University of California
Berkeley, CA 94720

The Folger Shakespeare Library
201 East Capitol Street SE
Washington, DC 20003

Freer Gallery of Art,
Smithsonian Institution
12th Street and Jefferson Drive SW
Washington, DC 20560

Jewish Museum Shop
1109 Fifth Avenue
New York, NY 10028

Lincoln Center for the Performing Arts
Gift Collection
140 West 65th Street
New York, NY 10023

Hansen Planetarium
15 South Street
Salt Lake City, UT 84111

International Museum of Photography
George Eastman House
900 East Avenue
Rochester, NY 14607

Library of Congress
Central Services Division, Box C
Washington, DC 20540

Metropolitan Museum of Art
Box 255, Gracie Station
New York, NY 10028

215

The Metropolitan Opera of New York
1865 Broadway,
New York, NY 10023

Museum of American Folk Art
55 West 53rd Street
New York, NY 10019

Museum of the City of New York Shop
Fifth Avenue and 103rd Street
New York, NY 10029

Museum of Fine Arts
Box 1044
Boston, MA 02120

Museum of Modern Art
11 West 53rd Street
New York, NY 10019

The National Trust for Historic
Preservation
1600 H Street NW
Washington, DC 20006

New York Botanical Gardens
Gift Shop
Bronx, NY 10458

New York Philharmonic
P.O. Box 5000
Ansonia Station
New York, NY 10023

Oceanic Society Gift
Stamford Marine Center
Magie Avenue
Stamford, CT 06902

Old Sturbridge Village
Museum Gift Shop
Sturbridge, MA 01566

Pierpont Morgan Library
29 East 36th Street
New York, NY 10016

Save the Children
Crafts Center
P.O. Box 990
Westport, CT 06880

The Smithsonian Institution
Mail Order Division
P.O. Box 199
Washington, DC 20560

South Seaport Museum Shops
203 Front Street
New York, NY 10038

Textile Museum
2320 S Street NW
Washington DC 20008

Winterthur Museum and Gardens
Winterthur,
DEL 19735

Specialty Stores and Mail-Order Sources

Abbey Press
63 Hill Drive
St. Meinrad, IN 47577

Abercrombie and Fitch
400 South Edward Street
Mount Prospect, IL 60057

Actor's Heritage
262 West 44th Street
New York, NY 10036

Banana Republic (travel and safari
clothes)
Box 7737
San Francisco, CA 94120

Books on Tape
P.O. Box 7900
Newport Beach, CA 92660

Brookstone Company (tools and
housewares)
5 Vose Farm Road
Peterborough, NH 03458

Burpee (seeds and shrubs)
2344 Burpee Building
Warminister, PA 18974

Caswell-Massay Co. Ltd (toiletries)
Catalogue Division
111 Eighth Avenue
New York, NY 10011

Childcraft Education Corp. (toys)
20 Kilmer Road
Edison, NJ 08818

The Chocolate Collection
P.O. Box 217
Paradise, PA 17562

Collector's Guild (works of art)
601 West 26th Street
New York, NY 10001

Comfortably Yours (aids for easier
living)
52 West Hunter Avenue
Maywood, NY 07607

Consumer's Distributing
205 Campus Plaza
Edison, NJ 08837

Day Timer Executive Gift Catalog
Allentown, PA 18001

Down's Collector's Showcase
2200 South 114th Street
Dept. 785
Milwaukee, WI 53227

Early Winters (unique outdoor
equipment)
110 Prefontaine Place South
Seattle, WA 98104

The Enchanted Doll House
Manchester Center, VT
05255-0697

Enticements Ltd.
777 Irvington Place
Thornwood, NY 10594

Funny Side Up (humorous gifts)
425 Stump Road
North Wales, PA 19454

Games
800 Morse Avenue
Elk Grove Village, IL 60007

Giggletree
Winterbrook Way
Meredith, NH 03253

Hamokor Judaica, Inc
PO Box 59453
Chicago, IL 60659

Hammacher Schlemmer
147 East 57th Street
New York, NY 10022

Harry and David (gift packaged food)
Bear Creek Orchards
Medford, OR 97501

Howard Kaplan's French Collection,
Ltd
450 Park Avenue - Suite 2702
New York, NY 10022

Innovations
110 Painters Mill Road
Owings Mills, MD 21117

Just For Kids
Winterbrook Way
Meredith, NH 03253

Lilian Vernon
510 South Fulton Avenue
Mount Vernon, NY 10550

LL Bean, Inc.
Freeport, ME 04033

Lynchburg, Hardware and General
Store
Lynchburg, TN 37352

Markline
P.O. Box C-5
Belmont, MA 02178

Mark Cross
645 Fifth Avenue
New York, NY 10022

Maxim's (country gifts)
2001 Holland Avenue
Port Huron, MI 48061

One Shubert Alley (theater-related
gifts)
311 West 43rd Street
New York, NY 10036

The Paragon
PO Drawer 511
Tom Harvey Road
Westerly RI 02891-0511

Playbill
Dept. TEM 3
100 Avenue of the Americas
New York, NY 10013

Poets and Writers
201 West 54th Street
New York, NY 10019

Potpourri (artistic household items)
Dept P125
204 Worcester Street
Wellesley, MA 02181

Products That Think
One JS&A Plaza
Northbrook, IL 60062

Scottish Lion
North Conway, NY 03860

Sir Thomas Lipton Collection
  (combined food and container gifts)
One Lipton Plaza
P.O. Box 2005
Nashua, NH 03061

Spiegel
1040 West 35th Street
Chicago, IL 60609

The Sharper Image Catalogue
  (hi-tech/new tech)
680 Davis Street
San Francisco, CA 94111

Steuben Glass
Fifth Ave and 56th Street
New York, NY 10022

Theater Arts Bookshop
405 West 42nd Street
New York, NY 10036

Think Big
390 West Broadway
New York, NY 10012

Williams-Sonoma (gourmet
  housewares)
Mail Order Dept.
P.O. Box 7456
San Francisco, CA 94120-7456

The Wine Enthusiast
70 Memorial Plaza
P.O. Box 39
Pleasantville, NY 10570

The Wooden Soldier (holiday
  ornaments)
North Hampshire Common
North Conway, NH 03860

Index

Babies, gifts for (*cont.*)
  Baby-Carriage Quilt, 35–37
  Commemorative Pincushion,
    43–44
  Crib Mobile, 31
  Hankie Bonnet, 29–30
  Name Pillows, 38–42
  "On the Day I Was Born"
    (scrapbook), 32–33
  put-together suggestions, 27–
    28
Baby Bead Bracelet, 34
Baby-Carriage Quilt, 35–37
Balloon pin, 75
Barrette and Jewelry Holder, 70–
  72
Basic craft techniques and tips,
  10–25
  basic sewing stitches, 14–15
  basic sewing techniques, 15–
    17
  decorative techniques, 21–25
  equipment, 10
  small soft-sculpture face, 18–
    20
  using patterns in this book, 12–
    14
  working with glues, 11
Basket:
  Bread Dough Breadbasket,
    171–73
  of Hearts, 205–207
  Herb Garden in a, 188
  Nest Egg, 141–42
  with Personalized Napkins,
    168–70
  Sunshine Sugar People
    Cookies, 194–95
  Welcome, 164–65
Bat Mitzvah gifts, 6

Beach Mat, 96–101
Birdseed Buds, 126–27
Birthday gifts:
  Birthday Box, 73–74
  3-D Birthday Card, 86–89
  Treasure Hunt, 119
Birth months:
  birthstone, 94
  flowers for, 93
Blanket, Small Picnic, 134–36
Bonnet, Hankie, 29–30
Box, Birthday, 73–74
Bracelet, Baby Bead, 34
Bread Dough:
  Breadbasket, 171–73
  Wreath, 180–81
Bridal shower gifts, put-together
    suggestions for, 121–22

C

Candles, Hand-Dipped Pressed-
    Flower, 191–93
Canvas Game Rug, 78–80
Catalogs, 8, 215–18
Celebrity Money, 102
Chocolate:
  Message, 204
  Pretzels and Fruits Dipped in,
    184
Clipping curves, 15
Clothespin Personalities, 150–54
Collage of photographs, 179
Commemorative Pincushion, 43–
  44
Cookies, Sunshine People, 194–
  95
Crayons, transfer, 24

Plume

THE TALK OF THE TOWN . . .

(0452)

☐ **HOLLYWOOD BABYLON II, by Kenneth Anger.** You'll just devour this feast of revelations that features names like Audrey Hepburn, Truman Capote, Elizabeth Taylor, Doris Day, Judy Garland, Frank Sinatra, Clark Gable, John Wayne, and so many more names whose faces you know so well, but whose secrets are now revealed in a way that you never imagined outside your wildest and most wicked fantasies. . . .   (257212—$12.95)

☐ **THE COTTON CLUB, by Jim Haskins.** It was the showplace of legendary entertainers like Ella Fitzgerald, Louis Armstrong, and Cab Calloway . . . it was the property of some of the roughest mobsters in Manhattan . . . it was the favorite haunt of everybody who was anybody—Ethel Merman, Irving Berlin, Fred Astaire, Florenz Ziegfeld, and so many others. Now, in vibrant words and vivid pictures, are the times, the people, and the magic of the Cotton Club.   (255988—$9.95)

☐ **MOVIE COMEDY TEAMS, by Leonard Maltin.** From Laurel and Hardy, to the three Stooges, to Abbott and Costello, here are the inside stories of Hollywood's unforgettable comedians. Writer-critic Maltin reveals their private sorrows and public triumphs, and colorfully details the high—and low—points of their careers.   (256941—$9.95)

☐ **AMERICAN FILM NOW: The People, The Power, The Money, The Movies by James Monaco.** Revised edition. Hollywood movies today are bigger—but are they better than ever? In this major examination of modern American cinema, one of our leading film critics ponders this question in a sweeping study of Hollywood today. (255457—$14.95)

All prices higher in Canada.

Buy them at your local bookstore or use this convenient coupon for ordering.

NEW AMERICAN LIBRARY
P.O. Box 999, Bergenfield, New Jersey 07621

Please send me the PLUME BOOKS I have checked above. I am enclosing $_____
(please add $1.50 to this order to cover postage and handling). Send check or money order—no cash or C.O.D.'s. Prices and numbers are subject to change without notice.

Name _____

Address _____

City _____ State _____ Zip Code _____

Allow 4-6 weeks for delivery.
This offer subject to withdrawal without notice.

There's an epidemic with 27 million victims. And no visible symptoms.

It's an epidemic of people who can't read.

Believe it or not, 27 million Americans are functionally illiterate, about one adult in five.

The solution to this problem is you... when you join the fight against illiteracy. So call the Coalition for Literacy at toll-free **1-800-228-8813** and volunteer.

Volunteer Against Illiteracy. The only degree you need is a degree of caring.